a strange path to freedom

White-Collar Professional Finds Inspiration and Gratitude in Federal Prison

HOLLY PASUT

A Strange Path to Freedom: White-Collar Professional Finds Inspiration and Gratitude in Federal Prison
By Holly Pasut

Designed, produced, and published by SPARK Publications
SPARKpublications.com
Charlotte, NC

Events described in this memoir are true accounts and recollections of the author's experience. Names of individuals mentioned throughout the book have been changed to protect their privacy.

Printed in the United States of America.
Paperback, May 2018, ISBN: 978-1-943070-37-4
Library of Congress Control Number: 2018936371

Dedication

To my three children, Rocky, Alexi, and Zico,
the reasons I kept marching,
every step just a little closer to home

To my only sister, Heidi,
who took me on as her full-time job
and became my kids' second mom

To my dad,
who picked me up from prison in a pink shirt,
and then I knew I hadn't disappointed him forever

To my mom,
who told me pencils have erasers because
everyone makes mistakes

To Alessandro,
the father of my three kids, who is deeply missed

To God,
who remained my foundation even when
I burned to the ground and lost faith

Table of Contents

Preface....7

SECTION ONE: Before Awareness

1 Life as a Successful Real Estate Agent....13
2 The FBI and Me....19
3 Plead Guilty or Go to Trial....23

SECTION TWO: Life in the Big House

4 Welcome to Alderson....37
5 My Cozy-Lumpy Bed....45
6 Finding Meaning....47
7 Shoes with Holes....51
8 Dinner Reservations....57
9 The Mysterious Lady....65
10 Feeling Sexy in Prison....69
11 Living a New Way of Thinking....77
12 Sunday Morning Daydreams....83
13 The Club....87

14 Gay for the Stay 89
15 Christmas Crocheting 93
16 Compassionate Payphones 99
17 The Ones Left Behind 103
18 Mail Call and the Pink Chain 107

SECTION THREE: Going Home

19 Trust 115
20 Dreams 121
21 Sipping Coffee with God 125
22 Inspiration and Wisdom 127
23 My New Year's Revolution 131
24 Intentional Listening 133
25 Mentally and Physically Free 139
26 God's Homing Device 143
27 My Final Lesson 147

About the Author 155

preface

This is a true story about the truths I discovered while serving a twenty-one-month sentence in federal prison and curiously contemplating how I—an educated, single mom with a thriving real estate practice—got there. I share personal thoughts and experiences at the risk of sounding like a highly unattractive fool. Some names in my story have been changed to protect those who wish to remain anonymous.

After my release from prison, I observed people around me who were actually free—without limitations on resources—behave and act as if they were tormented. Mentally, they voluntarily caged themselves. A counselor in prison used to tell my fellow inmates and me, "You are not that important." The *less important* I became, the more I explored new ways to see and to hear, and that gave me a new freedom, a greater freedom.

Finding emotional freedom while I was physically sent to prison was a gift. I believe some favors are to be shared and left behind for others in need. We all spend time in prison in some form—physically, emotionally, or both. All too often it's a prison of our own making. Clearly, I do not want to return to prison nor do I recommend it to you, but I am strangely grateful for the experience. And some routes to freedom are much better than others.

Alessandro, my husband and the father of my children, committed suicide when our youngest child was nine months old. *I will never understand why*. I fought anger toward him for many years, and even today it creeps in. But he did leave me with three gorgeous, strong-willed, and loving children, and I see his face every time I look at them. I raised them the best I knew how—not as victims, but as overcomers. I often share stories about Italy and how funny he was. I cannot help but miss him. I told the stories about him to the ladies in prison, who loved how I impersonated his Italian accent. It made the stay a little more tolerable.

My mother also committed suicide, but *I do understand*. Her mind was alert, but her body was failing due to chronic fatigue syndrome. She told me she felt like a prisoner in her own body. I don't condone suicide as a method to freedom. It only creates more suffering for those left behind. But for my mom, at least I understand why.

My past journeys have convinced me that pain and suffering are usually neither fun nor fatal. (I absolutely prefer fun.) I also discovered hope and love, which usually comes after the pain and suffering. Opposites attract.

You and I, however, are more alike than different; we recognize each other's love at our core. I want love, and I know you do too. Your love and my love can be friends. Together we can recognize and honor the divine light in one another. And if you find yourself imprisoned—literally or otherwise—know that you can find freedom. All it takes is a little optimism and inner strength, a willingness to move beyond the suffering, and a desire to find meaning.

I am still a work in progress, slowly coming to accept I might be progressing the rest of my life. If you have life figured out or you have "arrived," perhaps you ought to write a book. We all have our own personal stories. Maybe our stories are for other people, and that is why some of us share them. I will go first. My journey starts with a test and ends with a teacup.

With love,
Holly

Charlotte, NC
April 2018

section one

Before Awareness

Happy, single, head
of household, sole
owner of the remote
control, and completely
jolly—that was Holly.

chapter one

Life as a Successful Real Estate Agent

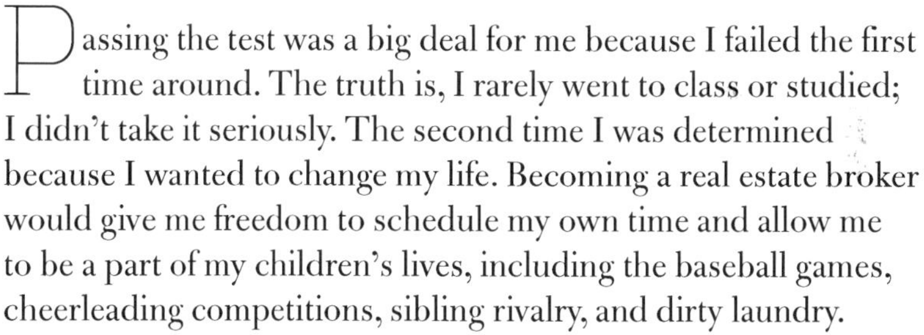

Passing the test was a big deal for me because I failed the first time around. The truth is, I rarely went to class or studied; I didn't take it seriously. The second time I was determined because I wanted to change my life. Becoming a real estate broker would give me freedom to schedule my own time and allow me to be a part of my children's lives, including the baseball games, cheerleading competitions, sibling rivalry, and dirty laundry.

Studying did not come easy for me. It was an undertaking. The house had to be quiet, but it was summer of 1998, school was out, and I had my three kids (two sons and a daughter) and their friends hollering and running throughout the entire house. Between the Cheetos fingerprints, television (which nobody was really watching), and blaring music, I was challenged beyond belief. My own screaming would go unnoticed, often to the extent that I had to exercise my own creativity. How could I calm the tribe and quiet the home? Cough medicine wasn't the answer, only my first idea.

The pool and pepperoni pizza became the babysitter for the entire summer. Logistically, I could see the kids playing in the pool and could monitor them as needed. Pizza kept them from slamming the pantry door, the home no longer rattling, and I could finally concentrate. Everybody was happy while I studied my brains out, overdosed on pepperoni, and gained ten pounds.

While turning the pages of my books, I fell completely in love with my highlighter. I held on to the bright yellow instrument for fear of missing anything important. I read, reread, answered all the questions at the end of every chapter, over and over, all day long. I was as equipped as possible for the test. After a restless night's sleep, a light breakfast, and a full tank of gas, I drove to Mingle School of Real Estate.

When most of the class had finished testing and left the room, I was still there. With every ounce of my brain poured into the test, I was satisfied and ready to turn the papers over to the instructor.

The instructor said she would post a "pass or fail" next to our ID numbers after lunch. We had at least an hour, so many of us went down the street for lunch. I had a glass of wine instead. Returning to the school, several students were walking back from viewing their results. Yikes, that meant she had posted them. If ever I could be described as timid and meek, that was the time. Slowly, I approached the test results searching for my ID number. PASS. *Oh, my God, thank you, God! I passed!*

Once I obtained my real estate license, I began advertising and marketing myself immediately. Marketing myself came easily for me. I had an instant brand.

It's no surprise, but real estate agents are often laughed at, especially when their ads are all ego. "I'm the best—pick me!" "I'm #1." "My dog and I will sell your home!" You've probably seen those nauseating slogans. (If you are a real estate agent reading this, oh dear.)

How's this one? "Who would help you with all your real estate needs? Team Holly-would!" Did I luck out or what? With a name like Holly, I couldn't resist. Advertising at the movie theater was a brilliant way to spend advertising dollars. I was instantly remembered.

One afternoon my youngest son, Zico, kept asking me if he could have something to eat before dinner: "Pleeeaaassse, Mom, three cookies? Just a few chips? A little chocolate ice cream? Can you order the pizza now?" My answer was no, no, no, OMG no! (If you're a parent, you know that answer.) Then he said, "I don't know why they call you Holly-would. They should call you Holly-won't."

I digress. Children will do that to you.

My life changed. The phone didn't stop ringing. Sellers wanted me to sell their homes; buyers wanted me to help them find a home to buy; and I was still trying to find my way around the office. I didn't know where to find contracts, addendums, or the stapler. Once, it took me twenty minutes to print an offer to purchase because I didn't know how to log on to the computer.

However, my entrepreneurial enthusiasm, energy, and dedication to being the best I could paid off. Unexpectedly, I was awarded Rookie of the Year, earning close to a quarter of a million dollars. The kids ate a lot of pepperoni pizza.

My business grew faster than I was able to manage. I was physically and emotionally drained. Struggling to sustain my listing inventory and assist anxious buyers was like trying to stuff a marshmallow in a parking meter. By the end of my first year, I hired a full-time assistant and found an additional real estate agent to help me with the overload of buyers. I was no longer a single real estate agent, but a full-fledged real estate team!

Juggling my three kids, a thriving career, and a dog that doesn't believe he's a dog is not for the faint of heart. That's why man invented vodka, wine, and take out. Despite the organized chaos, I loved my life. I remember going to bed each night looking forward to sleeping quickly, so I could get up the next day and start over again. Happy, single, head of household, sole owner of the remote control, and completely jolly—that was Holly.

My assistant was a team player, a friend, therapist, errand runner, deliverer of homework, which was often left at home, and gay. He helped me hang curtains, made wonderful coffee, and wrote the best Match.com profile any husband ever could. (I suppose asking your husband to write your Match.com profile would be crossing the line.) He was everything I needed in an assistant.

Monday mornings were made for exchanging stories of our romantic lives or lack thereof. It was not uncommon to see us laughing so uncontrollably we had to push away from our computers. But I could tell when he was sad, especially when his heart was hurting. Many times, I shared my own heart. Mine came with tears.

The weekends were crammed with a variety of social activities, from attending baseball, football, and cheerleading to sipping martinis in upscale restaurants and shopping with girlfriends. Shoes always had a way of improving my spirits, especially when they would call to me—"Holly, try me on! You'll love me! I'm sexy and hot and come in a variety of popping colors! You deserve me!"

While other people worshipped together on Sunday mornings, my Sundays were reserved for sleeping. I did not grow up with any religion and went to church only a few times. Sadly, my children had not been exposed to church either.

One Sunday morning, a friend, Patty, called me and asked if I would like to go to church with her. I said yes. I thought it would be fun to go to breakfast afterward, although I was tired and a little dizzy from a late night.

We were escorted to our seats, not pews but cozy theater-style seats. The band took the stage, which was creatively set with beautiful lights and images. The music was nothing like I had imagined. The sounds, the voices, the words—I could feel something inside of me. There was power in the music, ripping an opening in my heart. I wanted to cry. The music stopped, thank God, and it was time to listen to the pastor. I became entranced with the message as the pastor explained the scripture while relating the stories to our everyday lives. He explained the message in ways I could relate, in ways I had never heard. My curiosity and desire to understand the bible only continued to increase as I developed an insatiable appetite for more.

Weekends started to change for me. When my friends called me in the afternoon to finalize our evening rendezvous, I announced I would no longer be joining them on Saturday nights. It was paramount for me to sleep peacefully the night before church. I wanted to be fresh with a clear mind (one without traces of alcohol) on Sunday morning. Patty and I continued to attend church together, and the message would stay in my heart all day long.

My normal morning routine began to change from zooming upstairs to my office to quietly awakening before the kids went to school, brewing my coffee, lighting candles, and sitting in what became known as my prayer chair. Reading, meditating, praying, and journaling—I couldn't get enough.

The kids began seeing a change in me as well as our conversations. For the first time, I was coming to understand the bible and the story of Jesus. The kids became intrigued with the stories I shared and, in time, wanted to go to church with me. Treating them to all-you-can-eat brunch afterward may have helped.

I volunteered to become a life group leader at church and was responsible for facilitating the discussions. (Dear God, please help me!) Learning about the Holy Spirit was fascinating to me, and my faith walk became stronger and stronger. From reading the bible every morning and highlighting my favorite passages, the pages of my bible started falling apart. I often met with one of the pastors from church, and one day while speaking with him in his office, he observed the pages of my bible fall to floor. He laughed and said, "Holly, now that's a well-read bible."

Looking back, I worked my butt off to obtain my real estate license in 1999, built a successful career, and sustained through the adversity in the economy. I had always been an overachiever, dedicated, and disciplined. Other than my family, real estate was my world.

Life as a busy real estate agent while single-handedly raising kids was challenging, but I loved it—the fast pace, meals on the run, celebrating homeruns and touchdowns, always encouraging and clapping at the cheerleading competitions, learning about lacrosse, and even paying for speeding tickets and fixing flat tires, but never without laughter and loving so hard it hurt. Our home was alive—energetic kids, pepperoni pizza, cleats, missing belts, dog leashes, hair ties, and Xbox.

And then it slowly started to change.

I noticed a badge
as one gentleman
opened his jacket
ever so slightly and
asked, "Is there a
private room we can
move to?" He handed
me his card. FBI.

chapter two

The FBI and Me

In 2006 and 2007, the market was fast and furious. If you were breathing, the banks would loan you money. I was selling oodles of big-ticket homes like monopoly pieces until the FBI suspected fraud.

Investigators questioned me about several contracts written on million-dollar homes I had listed. They suspected the contracts could be fraudulent and wanted to alert me. I explained this to the sellers and told them I did not want to be a part of the transaction, especially if the authorities smelled fraud. The sellers were beyond furious to hear their contracts could be the beginning of a fraudulent transaction but regardless of FBI opinion, they didn't care and eagerly wanted to close. Because they didn't feel they were personally committing fraud, they saw no reason to terminate their purchase contracts (classic irrational thinking). On the flip side, I was petrified to proceed and kindly told my clients I would be unable to represent them. Then I studied fraud.

Real estate pre-licensing classes did not include "How to Detect Mortgage Fraud 101." (This has since changed, and there are now classes regarding fraud.) However, I did know how to list and sell homes along with the necessary steps for a successful closing. I loved teaching myself how to market and advertise like a rock star, but I did NOT know how to find fraud. I never suspected, not then anyway.

After some time, I developed an uncertainty about some of my own clients' past transactions. I began to feel I might have been a part of fraudulent transactions involving people I knew and trusted. After explaining this to my broker, who is the person "in charge," I suggested we call the FBI to let them know. She decided it was not a good idea, and if the "blue suits" wanted to talk to me, they would find me. You could have knocked me over with a feather when I heard her say no. Even though her decision didn't feel right to me, I listened to her instead of my gut. She was the "broker in charge," and I thought she knew best, so I took her advice.

One day, she called me into her office to question me about some contracts the FBI had questioned her about. After I explained everything, she didn't seem overly concerned. I felt the opposite and extremely alarmed due to the gossip I was hearing on the streets. The national news was unveiling fraudulent activity with the sound of a new jargon, as in straw buyers, inflated appraisals, and quick flips. Feelings of disorientation blurred my thoughts while I struggled to stay focused. It was unlikely this would go away. Slowly but surely, I felt something sketchy was unhinging.

After wrestling with uncertainty, I hired a real estate attorney and asked for a review of my contracts. I was panic-stricken because *I knew I did something wrong*. Licensed Realtors are not permitted to pay a referral fee to another person unless they too are licensed. I screwed up, and I paid a referral fee to somebody who was not licensed. He said it was not a referral fee but cleverly called it a "consulting fee." Nevertheless, I stupidly agreed to pay him. Have you ever felt someone was smarter than you? I thought he was an astute businessman, successful entrepreneur, and my friend.

My real estate attorney and I scheduled a conference call with the North Carolina Real Estate Commission. Even though I was putting myself in a jeopardizing situation, I wanted to know if there was more to my story. I knew the commission would be rendered speechless once they heard about the "consulting fee." I was prepared to get the beating of my life, even my license revoked. But I had to know if there was something I couldn't see.

I could hear breathing on the other end of the phone while I shared every detail about every file that gave me involvement. If only there had been an eject button, I could have launched myself through the roof. There were grueling questions and agonizing pauses of nothing but breathing space as I painstakingly and authentically answered their questions. I knew how foolish I appeared.

The conference call ended, nothing happened, and I continued practicing real estate.

After the brutal real estate crash in 2008, I joined another well-known firm. Agents were unable to sustain the drastic change in the economy and were eagerly searching for ways to reduce expensive overhead. Cash was king, and everyone was trying to keep theirs.

I felt it was only right to tell the new firm about my lingering FBI excitement, in case they thought differently about having me join their team. The broker was not jolted about my concerns but assuredly confident for my future success. Year after year, I was the top-producing agent—business as usual.

Let's fast-forward a few years.

The receptionist bent her head into my office and said, "Holly, someone is in the lobby for you." "Hmmm. That is strange," I thought. I didn't have any appointments, and it was rare for someone to just pop in. I walked into the lobby and laid eyes on two attractive men, well groomed and dressed rather nicely in blue suits.

"Hello, I'm Holly," I said as I reached out to shake their hands.

I noticed a badge as one gentleman opened his jacket ever so slightly and asked, "Is there a private room we can move to?" He handed me his card. FBI.

I blurted out my first thought. "Oh, my God! My kids?"

"Is there a conference room where we can sit?" he said.

The three of us moved to a small, private room. One of the agents asked if I knew a particular person—the man to whom I had paid the referral fee.

"Yes, I know him. Why?"

"Ms. Pasut, we suggest you hire a criminal attorney."

"What?! Why? Ask me whatever you want to know."

They asked me a few questions and asked if I knew some other names, which I didn't. As they stood up to leave, they reiterated I should hire a criminal attorney.

I never thought about how people react to shock. It was odd. I slowly walked back to my office and tried to finish my work. I was in slow motion, reminding myself to breathe, knowing I hadn't died but consciously aware I was not present in my body.

"Holly, get a grip, you are not a criminal," I thought. Needing help, direction, comfort, a stiff drink, a vacation, and wanting to disappear, I went to speak with my manager. She remained calm as a cucumber and assured me everything would be all right. She began sharing stories and experiences she had gone through, explaining how she and her husband suffered but came out on the other side. I was struck by her vulnerability and honesty, but I suppose knowing I had personal troubles made it easier for her to share hers. I guess that's why they say misery loves company. She kindly gave me a handful of criminal attorneys to contact.

I went home immediately but don't remember driving there. Sitting at my computer, the search began. What do you look for in a criminal attorney? It was my first experience; I was nauseated. The first person appeared to be the most aggressive—a fighter and a Christian. It felt like the best one.

The first appointment with my defense attorney was horrible. "Oh my god," I thought. "I hired a criminal attorney. Who does that? Criminals!"

chapter three

Plead Guilty or Go to Trial

My attorney explained, "If you go to trial, you will probably lose and spend many years in prison. If you plead guilty, there's a strong possibility you may avoid active time, or if you are sentenced to prison, it would not be very long, maybe only few years."

"Only a few years?" I asked. I preferred door number three. "Can't I talk to the prosecutor? Can't I answer some questions? I will tell him everything I know. Why won't he talk to me like a normal person?" I wanted to cooperate in any way possible, but I did not want to plead guilty nor did I want to go to trial. I needed to toss a coin: plead guilty or go to trial. Which poison was safest to drink? What if I lost at trial and went to prison for eight to ten years? What about my kids? Holly, be rational!

My attorney told me he was going out of the country for a much-needed family vacation and would discuss my decision upon his return. While he was sipping wine and sampling cheese in Europe, I decided not to plead guilty but to do what any other red-blooded, scared, single mother would do. I hired another attorney. How wonderful—now I had two attorneys on my payroll with hopes of getting double the work, better results. Tick tock.

Days, weeks, and months turned into years and years of waiting—waiting for the FBI and my life. Then the day came; my attorney called and wanted to speak with me, in person.

"Why can't we talk over the phone?" I asked. "Please tell me what you want to tell me."

My additional attorney, the one I hired while my original attorney was traveling through Europe, said he would be more comfortable if I came to his office. I lived in Charlotte, North Carolina, and his office was in Winston-Salem. This will be an all-day appointment. My sister and I nervously drove to Winston-Salem, praying it would be good news. I was extremely wrong.

"Holly, it is time to make a decision," he told me. "You would probably go to the same place Martha Stewart went. It's not too bad. You can drive to West Virginia and look around"—as if the prison were holding an open house. The drive home was overly distressing for me. Crawling into the back seat of Heidi's car, I buried my face and cried instead.

I scheduled time with my pastor the following day in hopes he could help me. We talked about trials and the turbulence surrounding people, and we talked about faith, believing in things unseen. My mind resembled a gigantic seesaw. "Will someone, please, please decide for me?" But nobody could be responsible for the decision but me.

I heavily considered going to trial and resting in faith God would see me through this mess. Yet the idea of going to trial was enormously frightening for me. The government rarely is defeated. I questioned myself: "Who would be more powerful—God or the government?" I don't believe I asked myself that question! Of course, God is greater, all powerful, sovereign and supreme, but could I take that chance? During the time of indecision, my faith wavered, and I sometimes felt I'd completely lost it.

My family and I ran through every scenario imaginable. "Holly, if you go to trial and lose, the judge will sentence per the guidelines, and your charges could warrant eight years," my sister reminded me. She would add, "I don't know, Holly. Maybe you should fight it. This is ridiculous."

"Mom, the government wins about 99 percent of their cases. You can't fight city hall. How long will you go if you plead?"

"I'm not sure," I said, "but my lawyer feels strongly I will avoid any active time."

"What the hell does that mean?" my dad clamored.

My attorney, who happened to be my third attorney, said if I pled guilty and cooperated with the prosecutor and FBI—"help them connect the dots"—the judge would be more lenient on me. The judge had his own discretion not totally based on the guidelines.

The voice in my head kept saying, "Holly, if you go to trial and lose, you're toast. If you plead, you have an opportunity to avoid active time. Listen to your attorney." I had to pick my poison because both options stunk.

Feeling dead and faithless, I answered, "Yep, I'm going to plead guilty. They win either way."

The North Carolina Real Estate Commission ensured me as part of my plea agreement, I could continue practicing real estate for fifteen months from the day I signed the plea. The commission could have easily revoked my license but decided to allow me this transition period. It was glaringly obvious I was not considered a menace to society! This stupefying decision was unheard of because the commission has the "right to revoke," which doesn't mean they automatically revoke. Thank God because as a single mother of three, I had no other means of support. How do I transition? How do I make a living and dissolve myself at the same time? I used my last months as a real estate agent to slowly disappear from the market and minimized advertising. It was most peculiar for me to get up each day to work on going out of business. I felt lost and lazy. I stopped seeking new business and assisted only those who asked specifically for me to represent them.

My father was born and raised in Williamsburg, Virginia, a West Point graduate and my hero. My sister, Heidi, and I were raised with discipline and a clear understanding between right and wrong. Dad prided himself on his love for our county and gratitude to our military—lover of the American flag, Scottish bagpipes, great leaders, and symbolic monuments.

Finally, that dreaded day had arrived, and in military fashion, my father stood tall as he insisted on accompanying me to the federal courthouse. I remember feeling numb, angry, but mostly hopeless. I was trapped in my physical body with no voice. I didn't need my father to discipline me this time. I could feel his eyes watching me from the back of the courtroom. All my life I wanted him to be proud of me. Our relationship had been marred because I couldn't stitch the wound of disappointment I caused. I wanted to die, again. Raising my right hand with my left hand on the bible, swearing to tell the truth, the whole truth, and nothing but the truth, it didn't feel right.

The media devours courthouse news and then immediately vomits it to the public. After only a few hours, my phone began ringing and dinging with emails and text messages. "Holly, I just read about you pleading guilty. You always treated my husband and me fairly, and we don't believe everything we read." "Holly, sorry to hear about your troubles. We will pray for you." "Holly, is this true what I'm reading about you?" I responded to everyone who reached out to me, thanking them for having the courage.

Once the news posted, people talked, stories started, and I became a prisoner in my own home. I wanted to vanish into thin air. The thought of sitting on my front porch and talking to the kids and neighbors, which I often enjoyed, was no longer pleasant. Too paranoid to walk to the end of my own driveway, I avoided going to the mailbox. Shopping at the local grocery store was like a bar—I knew most everyone. Now I'd rather starve than face the pain. Stale crackers were becoming an acquired taste.

Halloween was approaching, and I feared nobody would come to my home for candy. My imagination created a scary story, and I felt like I was playing the part of the ugly witch. Feelings of despair and shame gave me no light at the end of the tunnel. My soul was dying; I hated my life.

My daily meditation and prayer was no longer filled with hope and faith but was unspeakable, regretful, and hollow. God saw me choose the government over him—what a slap in the face. I wanted to speak to God, but I was too ashamed at what I had done. The idea of pleading guilty and loss of reputation became less important to me, but the thought of aborting God was too draconian a punishment to bear.

The anticipation of not knowing if I was going to prison was overwhelming and grating on me, leaving me mentally and physically exhausted. Happy hour could not come early enough; therefore, my bar opened at 4 p.m. with a chilled vodka martini with three olives in a Waterford crystal glass or a bottle of Montepulciano. Salute! Alcohol became my pacifier, my soothing mechanism, my new friend.

I never suspected I was drinking heavily; I functioned daily and was productive, as productive as anyone could expect to be after pleading guilty and being publicly shamed. With a degree in physical education from Florida State University (many moons ago), health and fitness have consistently been a part of my life—it's who I am. I continued my normal diet and daily exercise combined with falling asleep very early. Friends said it was unusually early.

The day I woke up in an ambulance and saw a stranger looking at me I thought, "Fantastic, it's over for me." Not really. I had no idea what had happened. The paramedic held my hand and said, "Holly, you had a seizure. You're okay." What the hell?

The neurologist came to the examination room and said, "The tests have confirmed what I suspected; you have epilepsy."

"Epilepsy? I read about that in the bible—those people were possessed. Oh my god, I'm evil," I thought.

The news got worse: "Holly, it is unlawful for you to drive. You must remain seizure-free for one full year before driving again. I want you to reduce your alcohol intake as well." I had not told the doctor about my legal troubles and wasn't sure I wanted to, but I did know I wasn't planning to reduce my alcohol intake—it was my daily joy. Transitioning out of real estate, commission checks were few and far between, my reputation had been tainted and aired, and now I was an epileptic coupled with the loss of my driving privilege. A real estate agent who didn't drive!

Before my grand-mal seizure, I enjoyed riding my Harley-Davison Heritage Softail—riding through the backcountry roads, savoring the smell of green fresh-cut grass and earthy hints of nature, aromas you miss when you're in a car. My Harley was black and chrome with a custom Corbin seat and black saddlebags, both fringed and studded. Two-inch bullet speakers were installed under my handlebars, just so I could crank up my music and drown out the world and its problems. Johnny Cash, Reba McEntire, and Shania Twain kept me company and made me feel empowered. I was now losing that to my seizure. It was time to sell my Harley.

My oldest son, Rocky was a huge Auburn fan and had been accepted to attend Auburn University, but I suggested he decline. I thought Auburn would be too big a college for him and felt he would do better in a smaller school. But that didn't stop him from buying three ridiculously expensive football tickets. These premium tickets were awesome, but the magical moments of a "first-time ever" would be our personal touchdown. This was an opportunity to sit between both my boys and watch a live professional football game. As fanatics, we were stoked.

It was Christmas Eve of 2011. Carolina Panther fans were enthusiastic to watch Auburn's former star quarterback Cam Newton battle against the Tampa Bay Buccaneers. The holiday hustle and bustle was in the air. Moms, dads, kids, grandparents, and lovers were excited and anxiously scouring to find their seats. Zico, my youngest son, lead us through the crowd as he plowed through the sea of teal and black jerseys. It was adventurous pandemonium, blaring "pump up" music, and bright stadium lights. I felt strange, as if I were having an out-of-body experience.

I woke up in the basement of Panther Stadium and was confused by an unfamiliar face. "Holly, you had a seizure. You're okay." As I laid there in utter disarray, not knowing where I was, overcome by fear and panic, I finally recognized two concerned faces, Rocky and Zico. "Mom, you're alright." With such disappointment and realizing they witnessed my grand-mal seizure, I said, "What about the game? Did we see it? Is it over?"

"Mom, don't worry about the game."

Adjusting to my restrictions was not as horrible as I thought. However, the doctor warned me not to bathe unless somebody was in my home. She feared I could have a seizure while sitting in my bathtub and drown. That was a bummer because I loved to slither into a hot bath to soak away the stresses of the day. Of course, I usually had a glass of wine. Now I had to find someone to babysit me while I languished with bath bombs and a cup of hot tea in my hand. Could be an opening line for my Match.com profile? Looking for a tall, dark, and handsome lifelong partner with understanding ... (shezzz).

Instead of asking people to drive me to one of my favorite shopping areas that included Off Broadway Shoes, Home Goods and Target, I would rely on myself. I would pretend I was in Italy and venture out on my own two feet. Except Italy is known for renaissance paintings, sculptures, and architectural excellence. It does not compare to anything within my walking radius.

I had to take measures to protect myself when I was alone. As peculiar as it was, I armed myself with a note that said, "If you find me, I am epileptic. Please call my sister, Heidi." I strapped on a fanny pack, for fear if I had a seizure, somebody might steal my purse. And really, who would want to steal a fanny pack? What wonderful thoughts to have before taking a walk. Ugh.

I suppose it's true—all good things come to an end. (Who said that?) But for me it did. My transition time had run out, and I had to surrender my real estate license. Now what? How would I support my family and pay my bills? This was a whammy of a shock, a true wake-up call, except somedays I didn't want to wake up.

The government had assigned a probation officer to my case. Probation officers serve as the community corrections arm of the federal court system. They provide to the court two important services: investigation and supervision. Knowing my sentencing hearing would be scheduled soon, the government wanted to make sure I was physically present (versus fleeing the country) and not harming myself. This was an immensely difficult and overwhelmingly stressful time for me. I looked forward to having a cocktail at four o'clock each day, by myself.

When visiting my counselor, I was asked a stupid question: "How are you?"

"Are you kidding me? How the hell do you think I am? I was hoping a truck would have run me over, so I could have missed this meeting."

The day I received the pre-sentencing report, I prayed it was a step in the right direction. Wow, I couldn't have been more wrong. After reading the report, without hesitation, I began making changes. I was told to review it and sign it. How could I sign something I didn't agree with? My attorney cautioned me not to be overly creative in making corrections. I halfway listened. Apparently, this was not a good idea, and the prosecutor became "unhappy" with me. I had no idea it was my job to make him happy! What about the truth?

At last the sentencing hearing date had been put on the court calendar. Regrettably, the idea I would strongly avoid active prison time had changed. It seemed the government had chosen to seek a sentencing term for approximately five years, due to my editing the pre-sentencing report. "What? What happened? Why? This can't be true. What am I going to do?" I thought. With the hearing date only one week away, I lost my renewed hope and wanted to die, again. This time my attorney was "not happy." I was grasping for a way to pull this together yet realizing I had no authority over my future. Who would be in charge—God or the government?

My breaking point had arrived. On the verge of collapse, I shamefully went to speak with my pastor who had been on this nightmare of a journey with me. In between smearing a runny nose and wiping tears all over my face, I began hyperventilating. I told him I could barely breathe, couldn't concentrate, was unable to sleep, and was perhaps better off if I could cease to exist. I had considerable doubts about my own faith and felt numb to everything.

He asked me to describe what a home looks like after it has burned down. As I imagined the splintered wood, ashes, black soot, and broken glass, he listened and nodded. Then he asked me one critical question: "Holly, what's left?" I knew the answer—the foundation.

Yep, I was the house, exhaustively burned down, broken, shattered, and unrecognizable, but one thing remained and was protected—my foundation. Nobody, not even the all-powerful government, could take my foundation away from me. An unforgettable afternoon revealed a pivotal moment in my life. Through experiencing an array of emotions, from angst, disequilibrium, and frailty to departing with a pocket-size bit of restored faith, I left believing that no matter what my sentence would be, it would not be fatal.

As a mother and only parent to my three kids, I felt it was my responsibility to nurture them and not sink to becoming a poor, pitiful victim. I prayed for strength and assured them no matter what, nobody could take them away from me. We would get through this; this too would pass. I was beginning to believe my crap.

The morning of my hearing, I practiced my every-day routine—sipping coffee in my prayer chair and quietly reading the bible, completely aware I would soon be leaving the home for the federal courthouse, but strangely relaxed with a sense of calm.

My youngest son, Zico, drove me in my red Mini Cooper. I couldn't help but laugh. Zico had pledged never to drive my car. He said it would embarrass him because he was such a big guy. That morning as he drove me, I don't think he was embarrassed but solemn as he held my hand.

Waiting in the lobby, I wanted to greet my friends, coworkers, professional affiliates, coaches, doctors, clients, friends of my children, and their parents who had become close to my own kids. People and family were there for me from Virginia, South Carolina, Georgia, and Florida, and a few arrived unexpectedly.

"All rise." It was beginning. I hadn't given much thought to what the seating arrangements would be in the courtroom. It was uncomfortable to sit in the front next to my attorney, especially when everyone I knew was sitting behind me looking at the back of my head. I could feel the tension and uncertainty of my future.

The courtroom had been scheduled for a one-hour hearing. However, that changed. The judge had mentioned several times how impressed he was to see the courtroom completely packed. In his eight years on the bench, he had never seen the room that full. Several people spoke as character witnesses, including my pastor, and a few professionals were asked to take the stand for cross-examination. As I listened to others speak about my character, I felt as if I were at my own funeral, only I was awaiting to find out if I was going to prison.

The judge decided to break for lunch and reconvene in one hour. My family and close friends escorted me to the break room, and we ate lunch from the vending machines sharing crackers and candy bars. I can't remember if I ate anything at all.

Returning to the courtroom, the judge commented how impressed he was to see most everyone had returned. The hearing lasted the entire day.

Everyone including the attorneys had spoken and made their cases. And then the judge asked if I wanted to say anything. I wanted to stand up and scream, "Hell yes, I want to say something," but I said, "Yes, your honor, I would." I remember standing up, looking at the judge, and asking him if I could turn around and talk to the people in the courtroom. I think he was surprised; he said yes.

For some miraculous reason, I could articulate, speak, and make eye contact with each person, feeling moved, loved, and supported. I expressed my gratitude for putting me on their busy schedules in the middle of the week, without pay, setting their alarms to be here on time, searching for parking—it was an effort, a true effort to be there for me, and I wanted to acknowledge them.

As I looked at my sister, I could see her disbelief this was happening. She was always the strong one, but this time she wasn't. This time I had to be strong.

My eighty-three-year-old father was trying so hard to be a soldier, but his eyes showed differently. As a little girl, I remembered him telling me to stay focused, determined, and to look forward. As I looked at him across the courtroom, I had a memory of a plastic card he gave me when I was a teenager, which I kept in my wallet. "When things get tough, the tough get going."

It was signed "Dad," not "Love, Dad," yet I knew he loved me.

Three beautiful young adults sat together, my daughter in the middle protected by her two strong brothers. When I saw them sitting upright, I felt so proud, the way they held each other's hands, even though they were scared stiff; I felt as if they would be okay.

It was stated several times through the hearing that I was a widowed mother and had the burden of raising three young children alone. I did not like that statement, so I clarified. Looking at Rocky, Alexi, and Zico, I said, "For the record, it's not easy raising a family, but never did I consider any of you a burden, but a privilege. Now, I want you to know no matter what happens to me, I will always be your mother, and don't try to get away with anything because I can discipline you from anywhere."

I turned around and faced the judge and then peered over to address the prosecutor. "You are known to be one of the best prosecutors, but I wish you had given me an opportunity to speak with you and possibly assist in connecting some dots, but that never happened."

Then I looked at my attorney, "Thank you for putting up with me and answering the same question over and over."

"Judge, thank you for letting me address those in the courtroom. I have been told you are a fair person and honorable judge. I have nothing left to say."

One man, a judge had the responsibility to decide my next steps. We adjourned and waited. At that point, I gave everything away. Whatever he decided, I was ready.

As we filtered back into the courtroom, it was the moment I had been waiting for. The English language sounded like Japanese to me until he said twenty-one months.

After the sentencing, the marshal escorted me to another room for photos and fingerprints. Does one smile for a mug shot? Apparently, I didn't. My fingerprints were very hard to detect. After about three or four attempts, they decided it was good enough. Had I known my fingerprints were so faint, perhaps I should've been a bank robber.

Returning to my home, I was joined by friends and family, vodka, and baked ziti. This support was undeniable as I was encouraged I could get through this. My "I" became our "we" meaning "we will get through this."

section two

Life in the Big House

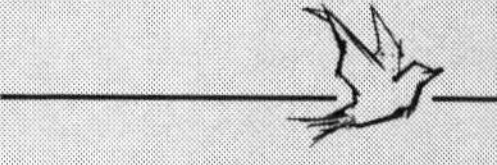

“Welcome to Alderson; welcome to living the dream,” the others would say as they passed by me. Seeing that I was barely able to breathe and most likely going into a mild form of shock, some ladies would pass me by and say, “Don’t worry. It gets better.”

chapter four

Welcome to Alderson

After the judge sentenced me to twenty-one months in federal prison, I was informed I would receive a letter in the mail regarding where and when to arrive. The longest I would have to wait to hear something would be four months.

Going to the mailbox caused an increase in heart palpitations and continued to be torture, although this walk of shame would evidentially come to an end. Oh joy. By my calculations, July 31st would be the last day for me to report somewhere. As it turned out, I was told to self-surrender on July 31, 2014. The absolute last day!

I rented out my home and moved everything into a storage facility. I took just enough basic clothing to my sister's house and lived with her until it was time to go—lying in the guest room, looking up at the ceiling, staring into space, telling myself I would be going to prison. Her guest room was unquestionably tiny, and I could almost open the closet door from the bed. Oddly I found this to be quite convenient. I also got used to the practicality of being able to select something to wear, easily, since I only had a few pieces of clothing. Simplicity does have its advantages.

Zico had also moved in with my sister and did not seem to mind moving his bed and personal items to a spacious, upstairs bonus room. It was one gigantic room. Heidi had turned it into a media room, but with Zico moving in, she made space for his king-size bed and desk. It was sad to see his clothes lined up along the floor, but he never complained. Truthfully, he was probably comfortable with stuff everywhere as it may have reminded him of his bedroom at home.

In the evening, I would go upstairs and watch movies with him, Netflix. We became hooked on the series *Breaking Bad* and nervously watched as Walter White dug himself into a deep hole. I could have watched paint dry; I didn't care. This precious time was almost worth going to prison for.

Zico is about six-foot-three, 235 pounds, and played college football. He is a gentle giant. We would take our spots on his bed, propping ourselves up against the wall, with our overflowing bowls of ice cream. Spending time with him was the highlight of my day. On the other hand, there was an unspoken mournfulness because we each knew there would be a night when these moments would be impossible.

One night while our eyes were glued to the show, Zico reached over and grabbed my hand. I froze, my heart climbed into my throat, and I refrained from looking at him, struggling to keep my eyes on the TV for fear I would fall apart. Even though I may have deserved to go prison, my child's suffering was my severest punishment. I had to look at him, and when I did, I saw tears in his eyes and followed them as they rolled down his cheeks. If ever I had preferred to be dead, that was it. His pain was unbearable for me to witness, more so realizing I caused it due to my poor decisions.

I was ordered to report to prison before 11 a.m. on July 31, 2014. Heidi, Rocky, Alexi, Zico, and I drove up the day before and stayed at the hospitality house in Alderson West Virginia. The house provides temporary lodging and support for those who have family going to prison or already been sent to prison. The dedicated volunteers on staff provide home-cooked meals, transportation, emotional support, and education. There is no charge, but donations are encouraged. We wanted to stay there because we had lots of unanswered questions and felt some assurance the owners would be able to guide us.

It was strange packing the car that morning. Nobody knew what to say or how to act. We knew this was not a vacation, yet with a coffee mug in my hand, my iPhone readily available, and dressed comfortably for the ride, it all felt too familiar. We tried to be positive, but we were headed for the unknown, feeling nauseated and frightened.

Once we found the hospitality house, we got a little excited, maybe because we knew we didn't have to drive any more on the twisting, curving, and turning narrow roads of West Virginia mountains.

Do not confuse Alderson hospitality house with the Four Seasons Hotel. From the street it looks dilapidated and haunted, even though it was clean and safe. And for the record, I never want to go back there again.

We stayed in one big room with three twin beds accommodating Heidi, Rocky, and Zico. Alexi and I slept in the one double bed. (Slept is an overstatement.) The communal bathroom was minimal, sterile, and certainly nothing like home sweet home. I felt like part of the Walton family—good night, Johnny; good night, Billy—except this time it was good night, Heidi, I love you; good night, Rocky, I love you; good night, Alexi, I love you; good night, Zico, I love you. Then I heard tears and restrained sniffles.

The next morning, we gathered in the kitchen for coffee and breakfast. I didn't know this would be the last morning for me to enjoy freshly brewed coffee in a ceramic mug. Nor did I know it would be the last time I sat on a sofa or a padded chair. This was the last morning for many things I had taken for granted.

Even though I didn't have to be at the gate until 11 a.m., the suspense of reporting to prison was killing us. I made my last free decision, announcing it was time to get the show on the road. We packed the car and drove to the prison gate.

I had received a letter telling me to look for the white phone and to pick it up; somebody would answer, and I was to let them know I was there. I said, "Hello, my name is Holly Pasut, and I'm early; is that okay?" "What's your number?" she snapped. "My regulation number is 27879-058." Why was she so moody? I was the one going to prison.

She told me a guard would pick me up in a few minutes and to look for the white truck. Then she said, "Say your goodbyes now."

I walked back to my family and said, "It's time for me to say goodbye." One by one, I said goodbye and felt as if I were slowly witnessing my own death.

The guard grabbed my paperwork and told me to get in the truck. She said, "Do not wave; do not look back." I knew my family was watching and waiting for me to look at them, but I was instructed not to acknowledge them, so I didn't.

As we drove through the prison gate, I was afraid and relieved: afraid of what lay ahead of me, but relieved I was going to finally get this over with.

The first stop was R&D, receiving and discharge. I had renewed hope when I saw the designated area for discharge. This provided assurance for me that someday I would process through those doors. That would be my focus!

The first order of business was for me to remove my civilian clothing and change into scrubs. One-size-fits-all, ugly yet cozy, and only temporary until I received my government-issued uniform. A female guard took me into the bathroom and told me to take off my clothes and put them in plastic-bag-lined trash can. It was a bit humiliating, but nothing like spreading your legs and putting your feet in stirrups to push a baby out.

I was standing completely naked in front of her, wondering what she was thinking. Then she told me to turn around, bend over, and spread my cheeks. "Now cough!" I read about this, but didn't think I would have to do it. I sounded like a baby lamb. Then she said, "LOUDER."

"Okay, tough girl," I said, "I'll cough. Oh my god, who would want this job?" She threw the scrubs at me and told me to get dressed.

After processing paperwork and fingerprints, she put me in a cell and told me to wait. "Hmmm, this is different, my letter didn't say anything about a cell. I hope they don't forget about me in here," I thought.

They took me into an administrative area to answer medical questions. The process amused me. The medical administrator had a little pinch of tobacco between his lower lip and gum. His resourceful spit receptacle was his empty water bottle, which was tucked to the side of his computer. I had a few medical questions for him.

By 2 o'clock I was getting hungry, thirsty, and mentally exhausted from days of anxiety. About that time, the guard took a few other new prisoners and me to where we would be living.

I fell into the rabbit hole as I walked into range B-1. I first noticed the concrete floors, dusty and dirty, and knew I wouldn't go barefoot for a long time. The row of payphones to my left was encouraging knowing I would be able to call home, but they were clunky, loud, and probably full of germs. I knew it was prison, but I am a germaphobe. Most of the women were wearing gray sweatpants with gray or brown t-shirts and flip-flops. Towels held up their wet hair. There were rows and rows of metal bunk beds. Welcome to the "bus stop," my new home.

The bus stop is typically a temporary place until a cube becomes available, which can take a few days or several weeks. It is adjacent to the bathroom areas; resonating sounds of flushing toilets, vomiting, and other mishaps are difficult to ignore. The overhead lights are bright and rarely dimmed, and sleeping under a florescent light is also a challenge. The bus stop is not only a temporary spot, but also a place for disciplinary actions. As a former real estate agent, I referred to it as the low-rent district. We all start there, and then it gets better! Woohoo.

My first night in prison, I remember it well. I had on the bright, florescent orange nightgown. This gown lacked the sexy style you would expect from a Victoria Secret special order. In fact, you might find it on a camping ground—my very own safety-orange, one-size-fits-all tent.

I almost strangled myself putting it on. Of course, I was in the bathroom since there was a door that offered privacy, which was not easy to come by. I exercised great control in that I didn't let any of my personal things touch the bathroom floor—so disgusting—which meant I had to scrunch the clothing up to keep it from dragging. I didn't want to include the hair of strangers on my sleeping attire. Once I got my one arm out of the neck hole and into the other armhole, I noticed I had the damn thing on backwards. Taking my arms back out of the armholes and spinning it around, then putting my arms back in the armholes, I almost got it right. But that one arm preferred the neck hole. I was frustrated and sad, longing for my own nightgown and the comforts of my own home.

This was not a maximum-security prison but a minimal security federal prison camp. Even though we were considered nonviolent offenders, I was not comfortable sleeping an arm's length from these strangers. What if someone reached over and strangled me? What if she was mental? What about sleepwalkers—if she started walking and then sat on me and squashed me? How would my family respond to that? I slept with both eyes open until I couldn't do it anymore. I prayed for God to rescue me, but he kept telling me I would be okay. I told God that was not what I had in mind. He laughed.

It was time to get up and do the morning cleaning, which consisted of making beds appropriately, military style, and sweeping the area and emptying garbage cans. To be totally honest, I didn't always make my bed at home. I felt very French that way. You don't get to feel French in *la prison*.

In case you don't know this, there is no Uber in prison. There isn't a Starbucks or wine bar either. You must walk everywhere, which I loved! The more I walked, the closer I got to home. Perspective, my friends. If I took the long way to the dining room, I could do a mile for each meal, easily three miles a day, and with my sturdy five-pound boots on my sore feet, I benefited from the added resistance.

I was recognized during my first walk all over the compound in prison. Not in a positive fashion like a celebrity—the scrubs identify you as a new arrival, and everyone stares at you. I felt ashamed, ugly, criminal, and punch-drunk. "Welcome to Alderson; welcome to living the dream," the others would say as they passed by me. Seeing that I was barely able to breathe and most likely going into a mild form of shock, some ladies would pass me by and say, "Don't worry. It gets better."

Today another lady
sleeps on the same
cozy-lumpy bed I did.
That bed is full of
mystery and untold
stories. I hope the
new lady in Cube 44
will find her magic
there the way I did.

chapter five

My Cozy-Lumpy Bed

When I was a little girl, my mother detested when people sat on beds. My sister and I could sit anywhere—the floor, a chair, our heads—but we were not permitted to sit on our beds.

In Cube 44, my home for the next twenty-one months, I had a few places to sit: the metal stool, which was attached to the wall and bolted under the matching, metal desk; the dust-ridden floor; or my cozy-lumpy bed. Filthy concrete would not have been my flooring preference; therefore, I pretended it was polished marble despite the floors being nasty and feeling slightly disgusting.

My bed was simply a mattress on a sheet of metal. It was ridiculously worn out from the many inmates before me. The springs had a way of finding themselves busting into my ribs. It wasn't until after pushing the springs back into the mattress and covering the hole with sanitary napkins that I found my coziness, which was not too bad. The tightly made bed became my one-of-a-kind designer sofa. It offered multiple uses as it served as my pull-up bar, kitchen, library, laundry room, and living room.

When I longed for privacy, my bed became my sanctuary. I could lie on my side and gaze at the Pepto Bismol pink cinder-block walls or on my back and stare at the metal bottom of the upper bunk—my ocean view or contemplating visions of my life to come.

Peanut butter and graham crackers never tasted so good as they did in prison. I rationed my supply until I could shop again. Springing onto my cozy-lumpy bed, I would revel in each taste while cautiously catching my crumbs, so I wouldn't have to sleep with them. Sitting up against the wall using my winter coat for added comfort, one slow bite at a time, it was gourmet *à la prison*.

Treating my bed as a library was a bit irksome for me at the beginning of my sentence. Unable to understand what it was I was reading due to the multitude of different noises around me made me crazy. Hearing ladies chewing on their potato chips, smacking their lips, laughing, singing, whispering made me cuckoo. After a while, I had to adjust and learn to tune out distractions that kept me from enjoying my designated library. A turning point arrived when my bed and I became a fortress. I would imagine I was at home lounging on my cozy, oversized chair, quietly sitting by the sunny window with my scented candle and lapdog. I actually read some of the most fascinating, transforming, and consequential books while spending time on my cozy-lumpy bed, books I might have missed had I not gone to prison.

Inmate watching from my bunk was similar to people watching at the airport. I could see everyone who passed by my door. (There really wasn't a door, just an opening in the wall.) Various women shuffled through the halls, never taking their feet off the ground. Some women advanced just under a sprint. I could see the guards looking in at me. Consequently, I waved at them sassily. It wasn't like they were going to put me in prison for that.

Today another lady sleeps on the same cozy-lumpy bed I did. That bed is full of mystery and untold stories. I hope the new lady in Cube 44 will find her magic there the way I did.

chapter six

Finding Meaning

Lying on my cozy-lumpy bunk, I stared up at the bottom of my upper bunkie's bed. The beds were gray steel with little holes in the bottom of the frame for ventilation. Through the holes, I could see her crumpled sheet and parts of her blanket. Seeing that gave me a funny feeling, as if something was going to fall through a hole. Sometimes her pen or book would fall off her bed and slide down the wall below onto my head. Almost knocked me out one time. I thought it would be frightening to be on the top, but a lower bunkie has her own cautionary tales too. I spent purposeful time closing my eyes to eliminate looking at the bottom of the upper bunk, but mainly to give me a different view, a view of my own thoughts. I was beginning to live a new way of thinking.

One of the firsts books I read in prison was *Man's Search for Meaning* by Viktor E. Frankl. In case you are not familiar with his book, it describes the suffering in the Nazi death camps while making some comparisons to our US prisons and discussing the effects of imprisonment. As a clinical psychologist, Frankl's primary conviction was that human drive is not about pleasure but the pursuit of what we find meaningful. I did find my circumstances unpleasurable, yet I was open to finding meaning in my mess.

Viktor Frankl wrote that whether in a Nazi camp or US prison, man will have common longings and desires. In one that particularly resonated with me, which I draw upon today, he said, "Forces beyond your control can take everything you possess except one thing, freedom to choose how you will respond to the situation. You cannot control what happens to you in your life, but you can always control what you will feel and do about what happens to you."

He was right. I couldn't change the fact I was on a crappy dirty bed in Cube 44, but nobody could capture my thoughts. I had regained freedom with an enthusiasm to discover meaning in my current situation.

This new awareness in having the choice to choose my own thoughts became a great friend. Certainly, I could have chosen my own thoughts before prison, but in prison, I *had* to change the way I thought. Even though I was physically locked up, I refused to be mentally locked up too!

The overachiever characteristic comes naturally to me, so with uncompromising determination, I decided I would not let any more of myself become captive to someone else, any policy, or governmental establishment. I was empowered to understand the richness in manifesting my own thoughts. However, it took a willful desire, an appetite for understanding, and most importantly, practice, practice, and more practice.

When my thoughts escaped my boundaries, I had to become a mentor to myself and reclaim healthier, rational thinking to relax and love myself again.

By continuing to draw upon some degree of inborn optimism, a sense of humor, and my precious times of solitude, I was given an inner freedom that shielded me from dangerous, negative, and hateful thinking. "Stinkin' thinkin'" was not going to incarcerate me any further than I was already.

I became skilled at choosing powerful thought. Sometimes I would break out in laughter. One of my most memorable thoughts was when I pretended I was filming a documentary as if my eyes were the camera. I would mentally record others' behaviors, entertaining myself and escaping at the same time. By changing my focus to observing others, it took my own pain away.

No matter what happened, how annoyed, upset, or lost I felt, I constantly took inventory of my thoughts to retain my sense of inner freedom. Suffering didn't control me, but in spite of suffering, I could navigate my own calculated thinking.

Finding meaning in my life today comes through searching. I don't feel I served time; I feel I served myself. The time was an opportunity to roll out my canvas and paint my meaning. It was my playground for spiritual growth and deepening, which I will always treasure.

"Yes, I would love them," I said. It was a day I would never forget—a running-shoe angel appeared. I felt like Forest Gump.

chapter seven

Shoes with Holes

You can only imagine the feeling when the guard gives you a pair of government-issued, ugly, black boots that weigh five pounds—steel toed, flat, bulky, and worn by many other ladies before you. I suppose had I dressed in short-shorts with a tool belt and a hammer, I could flaunt a little female sizzle, but black boots with khaki, elastic-waisted pants lack sex appeal from all angles.

The only way to move from one place to another in prison is to walk—up the hills, down the hills, around and around. And we all need proper exercise, no matter the circumstances. Regular workouts were part of my lifestyle before prison. But those bulky black boots were hardly conducive to working out. When I was a child, my dad encouraged me not to focus on pain or injury, but to focus on how great I would feel when the pain was relieved. In prison, I tried not to focus on my tired feet and oozing blisters, but the more I tried to forget the pain, the more I couldn't forget the pain! There were days when I was too-too pooped, and I would stumble over my own two feet. But the more miles I walked and stumbled with my ugly black boots, the closer I was to going home.

I desperately missed my multicolored Asics that were sitting on my sister's closet floor in Charlotte. Asics are incredibly durable and offer a standout gel cushioning system, optimizing shock absorption. They also glow in the dark to maximize nighttime safety. (Personally, had I chosen to escape, my Asics would have been my first choice in footwear, despite the glow.)

The women in prison who had running shoes had a different attitude. They seemed peppier and lighter on their feet with renewed energy. They had swag. A lady with running shoes was respected as if she earned her stripes, similar to a soldier who battles through the suffering and misery to conquer those damn black boots. The other hurdle into owning a pair of running shoes is having enough money to buy them. I had to prioritize the way I managed my commissary account. Save, save, save. Commissary spending was once a week, and most women bought chips, coffee, or candy. Even though I was craving more peanut butter, I wanted shoes that didn't hurt me. Someday, I too would join the ranks of inmates with their own speedy running shoes.

One afternoon in late September, as I slugged around the compound feeling like a rookie in my boots, an elderly lady walked up to me and asked if I needed some running shoes. I had never spoken to her before. At first, I thought she wanted something from me. It was prison, you know. I had been warned to watch out for people like her. I told her I was saving my money to order some shoes soon. Then she told me she had worn out her running shoes and wanted to know if I wanted them before she offered them to someone else. She guessed my shoe size correctly and knew her used running shoes would fit me. It was meant to be. "Yes, I would love them," I said. It was a day I would never forget—a running-shoe angel appeared. I felt like Forest Gump.

My beautiful, new-to-me running shoes felt like marshmallows compared to my boots. I felt normal, springy, even stronger. I was faster and had officially become "one of them," a member of the club. Prison was becoming more tolerable; I could walk without pain while noticing the beauty of the mountains, taking in the fragrance of trees and fresh mountain air. I felt the thrill of victory and no more agony of d'feet!

Before long, my worn-out running shoes and I became very close friends. Having lived a long, hard life, my running shoes were special and unique, with several holes on the outsole and on top of the toes. I looked forward to slipping my "holy" running shoes on my tired, aching feet.

The holes on the top of the shoe were a particular benefit, a built-in cooling system that worked quite efficiently in the hot temperatures of West Virginia. They were reliable, expansive at times, and odor free.

The holes on the outsole had their own personality. They collected bits and pieces of nature as we walked. Later, I would find small objects snuggling inside my shoes—tiny pebbles, clumps of grass, or plain ole dirt, sometimes a perfect trifecta. The most memorable goodies my running shoes gave me was sound. I didn't notice it at first. One rainy day, the sun came out, and I meandered around the compound to join the other women on the wet track. I noticed a sound beginning to resonate from my feet—squish, squish, squish, squish. I couldn't help but laugh. The squish-squish sounded like flatulence.

Since I can remember, I have loved shoes. I laugh every time I read the plaque hanging on my office wall: *I can handle anything as long as I have the right shoes.* This shoe fetish is not unique to me. Shoe mavens come in all genders, religions, races, and cultures. Folks with opposing political agendas often find themselves gathered at the same shoe racks (probably arguing over the same pair of shoes).

Shopping for shoes is one of my happy places, strolling around the shoe department being waited on hand and foot as if I am part of the royal family. It doesn't matter how much the shoe costs or whether I can afford it; it's fun slipping on as many pairs of shoes as I can find in my size. Flats, heels, boots, ballets, sandals, clogs, platforms, wedges, strappy, buckled, lace-ups, peep-toes—I love them all. I can't help it. My heart races, and every sparkle has my name on it.

Shoes are powerful. They can make us look sexy, successful, or homeless. Shoes can make or break the outfit. They can change the way you feel, from depressed to joyful, from unattractive and frumpy to gorgeous and in demand. The right pair of durable, well-cushioned shoes can prevent headaches, toothaches, and backaches. Shoes are forgiving and loyal, always there for you no matter how much weight you have gained. (Skinny jeans are quite the opposite. They are temperamental and come with high expectations. Skinny jeans are set in their ways and expect you to remain as you were on the day you bought them. How one sided and boring.)

Shoes offer grace and good looks to women and men alike. A man with a nice pair of Italian leather shoes makes my heart race. A man with style and courage will grasp my attention immediately—a man with the strength to walk into a room wearing red suede shoes.

A neglected pair of shoes sadden me, like those abused puppy commercials. Sometimes I feel sorry for my old shoes that have been beaten and scuffed as they lie on the closet floor. It pains me to throw the worn-out shoes away. They help me remember wonderful nights out dancing, wild concerts, and those long hot days while I was tending my garden. Shoes understand that their life expectancy is seasonal, and no matter how old they become, they have a way of embracing your foot and making it feel at home.

You have to admit there's something special about killer heels. What is it? Despite the pain and suffering, my feet endure, and I buy them! Price is rarely an issue if the shoe is screaming hot. It's not a question of whether I can afford to buy those sassy heels; it's can I afford not to? To all the heels I haven't worn, which still sit on my closet floor, don't worry; *someday I will wear you.*

What is it about those horny heels? You know exactly what I mean—the heels you wear regardless of what your clothes look like, the heels you slither in while wearing your birthday suit. The bedroom lights stay on when you're wearing the hormone heels. There will always be something doggone fascinating about the power of the horny heel.

Is it a sculptural, visual thing? The lengthening of the leg? The boosting of the booty? A woman's tush in a tight-fitting dress unarguably has more drama and punch if she's in high heels—racy, steamy, and spicy, all wrapped up in a pair of shoes! Men watch her sashay across the room and visualize capturing the prey before it gets away.

To all the men who love women in high heels, you ain't seen nothing 'til you see 1,200 women strutting around the track wearing gray sweatpants or knee-length shorts and stinky T-shirts with hair arranged on top of their heads—their worn-out running shoes instilling strength, dedication and perseverance. Now that's sexy!

Nothing can replace the excitement and adrenaline I felt when I slipped on my first pair of running shoes at Alderson Federal Prison Camp. Prison taught me a different way to look at shoes. I write about how shoes can make you feel sexy, skinny, and in demand. But truthfully your attitude will make the shoes. While my ugly running shoes got uglier and uglier, my attitude got better and better.

I have a new plaque on my office wall now: *I can handle anything no matter the shoes.*

One of my favorite
parts of working in CDR
was serving the wine.
“Red or white wine
today?” I would ask.

chapter eight

Dinner Reservations

The first two weeks in prison are for your orientation. Imagine your first day on the job as human relations takes you through the ends and outs of the corporate structure, except we did not have cookies and coffee at the back of the room. Even in prison, there are classes, handbooks, and tours. This way the inmate will come to know and understand what is required. I liked this part—it was crucial to get off to a good start. I was determined to be a good felon but cried all the time.

The first session began at 8 a.m. in the TV room. The room was not only for TV but also for ladies gathered in small groups to crochet or play cards. Dirty looks and trash talking were typically expected once the guard would request everyone to clear the space for our training: "Rookie Training 101." They hated us. During our training we watched movies about life in prison or documentaries about Alderson Federal Prison Camp history. Did they really think I cared about the history? I wasn't preparing to spend my life there.

Prison classes, including our orientation, was inmate driven, meaning inmates taught the program. Don't think special teachers show up to improve our lives. We learned from one another. Based on my observation, these ladies performed just like perfect role models. It was easy to see how serious they became, as if it were going to be their new careers. Hmmm, maybe it was.

There was one lady in the class who seemed to consistently raise her hand with questions. They say there are no stupid questions, but I disagree! This new arrival was probably in her thirties, a single mother, charged with a white-collar crime. (That sounds like me, but I'm double the age. Yikes.) She sat in the front row, geographically suitable for suck-up status. I suppose it's best to aim to become a felon with congeniality versus a felon without. I kept reminding myself how hard it was to find this kind of entertainment, but I was still in disbelief I was in prison.

The importance of finding a job was mentioned repeatedly. Find a job! Find a job! Jobs paid approximately $5.25 per month (yes, I said $5.25 monthly) and ranged from cottage maintenance (house cleaning), recycling, power house, plumbing, landscaping, recreation, and chapel to education and dog training. But the kiss-of-death job was CDR, the central dining room.

Most new inmates land in CDR. The hours are the longest, and in between shifts, you cannot read, nap, knit, or exercise—nothing. You have to sit at a table and do nothing. Nothing. Doing nothing after a few minutes is exhausting. This did not sound appealing to me, and I was determined to find a job before I got assigned to CDR.

Let me explain a few terms to you. You need to understand the word "cop out." This is a form used if you want to get an appointment to speak to a guard who oversees a particular department. Once the form is reviewed (which can take months), you will be placed on a "call out."

A call out is a printed sheet delivered to each range. It's important to review the sheet every day and check to see if your name's on it. Call outs are priority, meaning you must cancel everything else to attend a call out.

Interviewing for a job in prison was very different from the life I knew. Step one: fill out a bunch of cop outs, walk all over the compound looking for the cop-out boxes for each department, stuff the form into the box, and then walk away. Interview completed!

I would write additional information about myself and why I felt I could be a contribution to each department based on my education or my experience. I came to learn very quickly; it did not matter. Actually, I looked like a fool.

Another term is "open house," but hardly like an open house in the neighborhood. As a former real estate broker, I was a bit sensitive to this term. There were set days and times scheduled for open houses, which meant if you could attend, the guard would be available to speak with you one-on-one during those times. Inmates would line up outside the door with hopes they would have an opportunity to meet.

It sounds like a good idea, but it was not unusual for the guard to not show up. Or the line might be too long, and you couldn't get in. Or just when you were about to walk in, the guard stopped early.

I thought working at recreation was a natural fit for me. I graduated from Florida State University with a degree in physical education with thoughts of become a great coach. Teaching exercise classes or sports was not foreign to me, so obviously I dropped off a cop out. But I never got a call out, and the guards never had open houses.

Landscaping, plumbing, power house, recycling, library, chapel, and then education were my other choices. It was finally a lucky day because I got into an open house at education and was able to speak to the "right" person. She told me she would hire me! Yay, I was getting hired into the education department. My job was to clean the faculty's bathroom. How exciting!

How dirty could the faculty's bathroom get, right? I was to make sure it was sparkly clean by 7 a.m. each morning, Monday through Friday—sweep, mop, wipe mirrors, clean toilets, take out the trash, and refresh supplies. After lunch I was to recheck and do it again. The guard signed my form, and it was official. News travels quickly in prison. I was hired in the education department and proud of it!

My next step was to drop the signed cop-out form into my counselor's box. Each inmate is assigned a counselor. I am not sure what the job of the counselor is—I can't even tell you the name of my first counselor because meeting him was highly uneventful, although my second counselor was fairly cool. I discovered he rode a Harley.

The point of dropping off the signed cop-out form was for the counselor to know I had a job waiting for me after orientation. I was relieved and no longer looking for employment. My starting pay was approximately $5.25 per month. After three months of working I would be able to afford a can of coffee and a small bag of chips.

When the call out arrived to our range, I quickly found myself in line with 130 other inmates to review it. It was fascinating to watch inmates review the sheets. Some were quick and purposeful as they scanned the pages looking for their last names (it's in alphabetical order) and walked away. Some would flip through the pages and then do a re-check. Were they double checking to make sure they didn't miss their name, or were they being nosy? It was the inmate checking not only her own business, but everyone else's as well. That was instrumental in spreading the gossip around the compound.

This inmate would stand at the horseshoe flipping back and forth through the call out. Up the page, down the page, turn the page, study the page, and study the page more. I'm like, "Are you kidding me? What is the problem here?" Meanwhile the others are just standing around waiting for their turns.

Of course, we didn't have Twitter, Facebook, or LinkedIn, but what we did have was inmate.com—another term to know. Inmate.com is gossip, rumors, and fantasies. If an inmate was getting released, a new arrival was coming, a job was changing, or someone moved to a hospital, it was all on the call-out sheet. In a matter of minutes, inmate.com would spread.

Before I could look at the call-out sheet, another lady came over to me and said, "Pasut, you are going to be working in CDR!" "What? No, I am in education." She said, "No, you are not. You start tomorrow morning in CDR."

I was shocked and confused. I did everything I was told to do to secure a "good job," and it backfired on me. What went wrong?

I went over to the education building and told the guard what had happened. She was neither surprised nor encouraging; however, she did call my counselor. Apparently, according to the counselor, he never received the cop out.

Welcome to CDR. My first day, I walked into the dining area feeling lost and beaten. I told them who I was followed by my regulation number. The guards don't care about your name; it's all about the eight-digit number. "Sit down," someone said. All the other ladies were staring at me—hairnets, aprons around their bellies, some with gloves on. If I could describe this motley crew, I would say "living dead" comes to mind first.

Inmates tend to size up other inmates very quickly. Being that I was in my fifties, Caucasian, appeared educated, and attractive, it was easy to pin me for white-collar. And on top of that, I was a minority among the prison population. I felt the majority did not like me. For some reason, I wanted to be liked in prison.

My assignment was to wipe tables off and, once the shift was over, to sweep and mop floors. I still don't understand why so much lettuce and tomatoes end up on the floor, especially when the most popular lunch is chef salad. But I do understand why the salt and pepper shakers are missing at the end of each meal. Resourcefulness goes a long way in prison. Why spend that $5.25 paycheck buying condiments from the commissary when it's easier to steal them?

I decided if I was going to work in CDR, I would try to make the most of it, although certainly not for the generous pay.

The front of CDR had windows viewing the other buildings, and once in awhile, you could spot deer. It was a breath of fresh air to witness something unusually graceful, especially in prison. From the rear windows of CDR we viewed a narrow, bubbly river with dilapidated trailers on the other side. (Reminded me of Walter White!) Whoever those campers were, they sure knew how to cook hamburgers and hot dogs. I could taste how delicious they were as the smoke trailed off over the river to our side of the world. Life on the other side.

Just for my own entertainment, I referred to the front of the CDR as waterview and the rear as waterfront. Once the inmates got their food, I would ask them if they preferred water view or waterfront. After a few times of acting like I needed to be transferred to the psychiatric ward, the ladies started asking me if there were any waterfront tables available. It was how we managed to make the most of our circumstances. Actually both views were very limiting, but you could see whatever you imagined.

I liked carrying the trays for the ladies who were in wheelchairs or used walkers or canes. They struggled often, and I knew I could make things a bit more comfortable for them, so I did. I'm not sure I was allowed to do that, but nobody told me not to. There was something about "do not rescue other inmates."

One of my favorite parts of working in CDR was serving the wine. "Red or white wine today?" I would ask. Very few women abstained. A few asked for vodka martinis, but most were quite surprised when I offered wine. And then there was always a table of ten that would ask me to leave the bottle! I did remind the ladies—tips were always appreciated but not permitted. It was a joke, of course.

Thursday was "chicken day" and quite popular—a very long line of 1,200 hungry, salivating inmates. Of course, part of my survival was my own entertainment. Once the ladies had their trays completed, they would look around for a clean table. I was very diligent about keeping my section clean and tidy. Not only did I wipe tables, but also I made an extra effort and wiped the seats as well. No mustard stains on my patrons' butts!

By this time, most inmates knew I was going cuckoo when I asked if they had reservations with us today. So they would answer, "Yes, we certainly do—waterfront for four, along with your best Italian bottle of pinot grigio." They learned to tip me with a smile, and I learned to like my job, making $5.25 per month.

Serving lunch and dinner was not a difficult job; the challenge was between the two shifts. After the sweeping, mopping, and washing dishes, we had to sit on plastic chairs connected to the table. We were not permitted to read, write, journal, knit, or crochet, and some of us had homework we were unable to do. We had to sit. Sit. Sit. Sit. And if your eyes just so happened to close, you could be disciplined for sleeping. It was absolutely exhausting and unbelievably boring. I would have preferred having my wisdom teeth pulled.

Prison may be referred to as a "correctional center," but I am lost as to what that means. If the idea is to train or educate the inmates, this was clearly done "incorrectly." CDR, was a classic example of denying us the ability to read, write, journal, knit, crochet, or do homework. This attitude didn't encourage learning, but many guards felt their role was to discipline. (I guess the judge's sentence wasn't enough.) For me, it was life at a standstill, a waste of human heart.

Even though it was the worst job in the prison, working in the CDR was the beginning of my own transformation and perspective. Serving others, strangers—OMG felons—was hardly anything I ever aspired to do. I felt like a failure, but it didn't kill me. I mopped floors very well. In fact, I created my own secret system, although one lady got mad at me for not mopping the way she did. I had to explain to her that we all had our own unique way of doing things, and if at the end of the shift the floors were clean, then we did our jobs. We all tie our shoes differently, we fold towels differently, yet at the end of the day shoes are tied and towels are folded. She stared at me as if I were trying to outsmart her. Awkward teaching moment.

Wearing a hairnet and plastic gloves really got to me. Not a look I had ever sported. I had pride in myself as a fashionista, a designer princess, someone with class and elegance. I learned the hairnet and plastic gloves were not what I was on the inside, but only props to help me see differently. Some of my best memories are of CDR, including those sexy hairnets and gloves, but mostly of all the characters who endured the least sexy job of all in prison.

I had to remind myself this was my life for now, not forever. It's strange, but through my pain, creativity and imagination sprung. I became my best friend, and my friend and I felt mentally free. I like to think a little wisdom emerged too.

My career path today is only a path; I don't know where it will lead. CDR was somewhat instrumental in my own freedom today. I realized that before prison, I judged myself based on how others perceived me. While in prison, nobody cared because we were all on the same level playing field. I learned to stop demeaning myself over the menial tasks given to me.

Even though I am starting over, I don't fear rejection or judgment anymore. Of course, it's human nature to say I don't want to be rejected or judged poorly, but it's also important that I do not do that to others. It's way over my pay grade! Having a higher level of awareness about my personal thoughts helps me to live with forgiveness and tolerance towards others and myself, and most importantly, with a quiet sense of gratitude and being.

chapter nine

The Mysterious Lady

She was an observer who spoke only with her dark, deep-set eyes. Her grayed hair was pulled back tightly in a low ponytail, accenting her jawline. Probably in her late sixties or early seventies, she must have been absolutely striking when she was young, although some of her beauty was in her mystery, which was quite evident. I suspected she was from another country, yet I didn't know where. She looked different, perhaps wise, and I wanted to meet her. But I hadn't seen her socializing with anyone inside the range, only walking from her cube to the bathroom area.

Prison is a strange place, and not knowing what someone's life has been like, it's best to be cautious when approaching them. Once I asked a lady in the bathroom, as we stood at the sinks, where her last name was from because it was so unusual. She almost punched me in the jaw. I made sure I never brushed my teeth next to her ever again.

The mysterious lady often sat at the picnic table staring off to nowhere. I decided to approach her there. I told her my name and mentioned we were in the same range. She recognized me and offered to share the picnic table. I didn't sense a slap coming.

I sat down, and she said nothing. After a several minutes of nothingness went by, I asked her where she was from. New York was all she said. I told her I was from North Carolina. It was like pulling teeth for information. The less she said, the more I wanted to know.

Her name was Pinkey. She was a white-collar offender with an ungodly long sentence. Originally from Romania, she had lived in the United States for over thirty years. When I asked her what she did for a living, she said she had been a consultant.

"Consultant for what?" I asked.

"A consultant for people."

Oh, here we go again, I thought.

Then she said, "I advised people for a living. I come from a family of fortune tellers."

Fortune telling was not an occupation with which I was familiar, and it was fantastically intriguing to me. Pinkey was tight lipped about her case, and after that I didn't ask much. Instead, I came to know her heart, at least her heart while in prison.

Strolling around the track after dinner was something I enjoyed. (I enjoyed something in prison?) Inevitably, I would see Pinkey sitting at an empty picnic table as if she were waiting for something. I would strongly urge Pinkey to walk with me because she needed exercise. "C'mon you can't sit all day," I would say. "Your butt will get too big for your bunk!" She would laugh and ask me to walk slowly. That became our daily routine—meeting at the picnic table, walking, and talking about our lives, husbands, kids, flower gardens, and her fountain that she so dearly loved.

Pinkey liked to talk about Romania, especially her father. She remembered him to be exceptionally handsome, and her eyes would light up when she spoke of him. It may have been the first time I saw her smile. Over time, I realized what I had originally thought to be mystery in her eyes was really enormous sadness. She was filled with darkness.

It's doubtful I will ever lay eyes on Pinkey again, but I will never forget her. She may not have been totally honest with her clients, and probably made a few people outraged, but at the picnic table she was my friend. Naturally reserved, stubborn, with a sense of humor. Some combination!

After I was trucked (it's prison, we don't get transported in BMWs) to health services from a twisted ankle, I noticed Pinkey's concern as she patiently waited for me to come hobbling out. Strangely, she exhibited nursing skills I was not aware she had.

Pinkey and I spoke about religion and spirituality often. She would ask me questions as if she were a child looking for answers. We developed our own routine in that she would ask me a question and it was my duty to bring back the answer. This gave me a mission, which was better than looking at thin air. Plus, she was not able to read English.

She asked me if I thought she would be reunited with her husband when she died. She wanted to believe they would be together again as husband and wife. Hmmm. I began my research.

"Pinkey, according to scripture in Matthew, Mark, and Luke, the most obvious answer would be no." Her olive skin tone looked white. Being locked up in prison can harbor a forlornness of spirit, and I only added to hers.

It's our inclination to desire the truth, and anything less is not sufficient. We then went on to discus more of what I learned. Another source said we would all be married to the same person as the bride of Christ, and Jesus will be the joy of heaven. Together with those we love, turn our focus to Jesus. We will see his beauty and sufficiency, and we will be happy and satisfied together with those we love, feeling no sense of disappointment. Meaning, if we are not married per se, there still will not be any displeasure.

"Pinkey, ask God; he is your source. We don't have the capacity to know exactly what heaven will be like, but I believe it will be awesome, and that is enough for me."

Then I asked Pinkey if there was any truth to a recent rumor: "Is it true if I die in prison, my record will say I escaped?" We laughed so hard, we saw each other cry. Pinkey and I smiled once again, knowing we would be okay.

I would place my brown
or black colored pencil
under warm water to
soften the lead and
gently line my eyes.
On the days we could
not get hot water, only
cold, I would have to
put the pencil in my
mouth and swish it in
my own warm saliva.

chapter ten

Feeling Sexy in Prison

Getting ready for a visitor in prison was like preparing for the high school senior prom. Preparations began days in advance. I always knew what I would be wearing on any given day—my regulation khaki pants and either the long or short-sleeve button up with a short-sleeve brown T-shirt underneath. I looked like a zookeeper minus the hat. But for visiting day, my uniform would be extra crisp and well ironed.

I never knew ironing could be this enjoyable. I ironed the night before every visit I had. Standing in line waiting for the ironing board was interesting to me—it's there I learned several ways to iron pants and shirts. Some ladies pressed creases in the front of their pants, and some didn't. I decided to take a survey. This ironing phenomenon was decided by generations: the older ladies liked the creases, and the younger ones didn't.

The regulation uniform was referred to as "programing clothes" and was accompanied by heavy black boots. But we were permitted to take off the five-pound boots and wear our sneakers for visits. (Yay!) Since my sneakers were white, I would easily wipe them off with water and toilet paper.

Perfume was not something I had, but who needs it! Instead, I would tear out sample perfume advertisements from magazines that were recycled through the compound and rub the paper all over my uniform and even my hair. One of the first tips I learned from the older inmates (that's code for women with long sentences) was to buy fabric sheets on my commissary day and layer them in between my clothing because our clothing stunk after laundry day. But I didn't want to smell like a fabric sheet, so I saved the perfume advertisements for visiting days.

The commissary was not like Sam's Club. It was a long, narrow room separated by glassed-in shelves of peanut butter, rubber bands, barbeque potato chips, tortillas, tuna fish packets, hair color, chocolate chips, instant coffee, dried milk, yarn, and sugar, along with an assortment of enticing nothings, such as mascara for a visit! I would walk around and check off things I wanted and then turn the sheet into an inmate working the counter. Then another inmate would gather up my selection, and a guard would ring it up. There was never any exchange of money. (We were criminals, you know.) The money was automatically drafted from my account.

Shopping at the commissary was highway robbery—talk about criminal behavior. I've never paid prices like prison prices. And if I forgot to request anything, too bad, so sad—I had to wait until the next week. We could only go once a week on our assigned day. I would tell the ladies, "I am going into town today. It's my shopping day. Woohoo!"

We had an area in the back of the bathroom called the "hair room," which was the only place you were supposed to brush your hair. Otherwise, there would be hair all over the range. (Best prison rule ever!) We had three hair bowls for shampooing, but I rarely used those as it was easiest in the shower. The hair room was full of giggling and primping, braiding and blow drying, curling irons, compliments, and a lot of whispering. Several ladies were hairdressers in their previous lives, some better than others just like real life. Some were great at braiding, others at "wash, roll, and set." But I have long, wavy hair and lots of it; I needed someone who could do a "blow out." I received a referral and booked her services for visiting day.

My hair was brown when I arrived at Alderson Federal Prison Camp, but over time it became very dark brownish black. The coloring products in the commissary were not exactly what I was used to in top salons. Color in a box meant "whatever color" in a box. When my "sparkles" (gray hair) started appearing, my friend from Brooklyn would be sure to let me know. (Who did she think I was trying to impress?) Sometimes I colored my hair just so she would stop nagging me.

Some ladies never colored their hair. Either it was a time for freedom and letting go, or they didn't have money to buy the color. You could measure the years someone had been in prison by the length of their gray hair. It looked like a big stripe.

Oh, the showers—they only lasted six minutes. If they hadn't been timed, I would still be standing in line today. Once someone comes out, the next person goes right in. I would have my cheap towel and bath bag with soap, shampoo, and razor. After getting everything lined up for easy access, I would press the button. There were no levers to adjust the temperature of the water. Just press the button and begin. The water was usually too hot, too cold, or sometimes a combination of both—starts hot and goes to cold. I felt like Goldilocks hoping to find the porridge that was just right.

What was really crummy was when the shower would automatically stop. There was no warning unless you took a watch in the shower with you. I preferred living dangerously, so I always guessed. But sometimes the shower beat me and I would be standing in a freezing shower with shampoo and soap all over myself. After the water stopped, you had to wait another six minutes before they would turn on again. I would stand there wanting to disappear. Then I would crack up laughing, thinking to myself, "If my friends could see me now." It was another lovely form of punishment—or maybe just bad timing. The other inmates waiting in line would become quite intolerant. I hoped by the time I finished rinsing and came out of the shower, a new group of women would be waiting in the line and wouldn't realize I had tied the shower up for eighteen minutes.

On to the primping. I look better with makeup on. Even though during the week I rarely wore any, I always did for my visits. For starters, I wanted my family to recognize me. And I didn't want them to think I was sick. Since there was not a variety of cosmetics to choose from, the inmates got creative.

One can do more with a colored pencil than you might think. Actually, colored pencils were big sellers at the commissary. I would place my brown or black colored pencil under warm water to soften the lead and gently line my eyes. On the days we could not get hot water, only cold, I would have to put the pencil in my mouth and swish it in my own warm saliva. That's called resourceful, not gross. The popping red and pink pencils were a must for the lips. I would soften the lead with extra attention until the color gently glided over my lips.

I loved the variety of colors to choose from. I could choose a peach for my cheeks, placing little dots on my cheek bones and then rubbing to add the blushing color to my face. The color stays on for several hours, and the box of colored pencils lasts a long time. That could be good news or bad news depending on the length of your sentence.

With my uniform pressed, hair blow-dried with bouncing curls, makeup bright and glowing, and smelling like a magazine perfume sample, I was ready for the red phone to ring. The red phone sits at the top of the horseshoe area. The horseshoe is a U-shaped desk area at one end of the range. There is one lonely chair only for the guard, a bank of drawers, and a few dusty shelves holding random clothing and personal items known to be the "lost and found." Believe it or not, women in prison actually turn in lost items instead of keeping them. Just because a woman is in prison doesn't mean she's a bad person any more than a woman who has her freedom is a good one.

The women who were expecting visitors generally stood around the horse-shoe waiting for the phone to ring. Every time the phone rang, I would get so excited even when it wasn't for me. Just watching the other ladies get their calls was exhilarating.

I would pick up the phone on the first ring, and the guard on the other end would say, "I'm looking for Pasut." I would say, "This is Pasut 27879-058." Then the guard would interrupt and say, "You have a visitor." My heart would jump. Until the call came, I never really knew what to expect. Sadly, I became so used to being disappointed and defeated over and over again that I learned to accept whatever life threw at me. Just because I expected a visitor, until the guard called and told me to come to the visiting room, I was always on pins and needles.

Walking to the visiting area is the most joyful walk of all—knowing my family had arrived safely from their four-hour drive from Charlotte and knowing they successfully cleared all security checks in order to be in the visiting room.

There is a special attire for visitors. Visitors may not wear open-toe shoes. Female visitors must wear a bra and may not wear miniskirts, halter tops, or see-through clothing of any kind. Who would wear see-through clothing to a prison? Never mind the question. No cell phones, food, or drinks can be carried in either. Most families were prepared with their baggies of coins for the vending machines.

I used to joke around with my boys, especially Zico because I started to think he came to visit me just for the peanut butter and jelly sandwiches from the vending machines. He would buy about five of them and have them securely gathered at the seating area. "Here, Mom. I have a sandwich for you!"

Monopoly was another visitor favorite, especially for my boys. Rocky and Zico would drive to West Virginia together and talk about how they were going to crush me in Monopoly. As a former real estate agent, I found myself getting overly competitive. Park Avenue and Boardwalk were only starters. It does sound strange to say, but we had great memories of our time together rolling the dice and collecting rent in the visiting room, despite it being prison.

Once I got to the visiting room inmate entry door, I would have to stand and wait in line to get checked. We weren't supposed to look at the visitors waiting in line to get in. They stood in the parking lot near the gate. Since we were always being watched, I didn't take any chances and stood with my head down. It was kind of creepy because my family could see me walking down the hill toward them, but I wasn't allowed to look at them—no waving or acknowledging them until I cleared all security.

The inmate door would open, and the guard would call me in the tiny room. "Shut the door." Just me and the guard. She would go through a checklist of everything I had on—hairband, bra, undies, socks, and so forth. She'd check behind ears and under arm pits. I'd spread my legs apart with arms stretched out to my sides, so she could pat me up and down. Then I'd turn around for another pat down. "Cleared. Have a nice visit."

Finally the visit! I'd open the door, and all the anticipation building up inside of me would dissipate into an emotional release of tears and hugs. I would be so elated to see my family, touch them, and look directly into their eyes. For a few minutes, there would be a strangeness as I studied them and they studied me. I knew I appeared different. There was no way around the shock of it all. But at least I had big, sexy curls and fake Mac lipstick.

Observing my sister's and friends' attire was like going to Vegas for me. I would start with the great jewelry and stylish clothing, move to the shoes, and end with the nail polish. It gave me so much joy to see and appreciate how other people looked and felt.

Sometimes we had a full six hours to visit, from morning to late afternoon. I found myself checking the clock often, not wanting the time to move. Just knowing my visitor would be leaving was too painful to imagine. I tried to cling to every word and gesture, capturing every minute as a photograph in my mind.

There was an inmate whose job was to walk around and take pictures. She would deliver them to our bunks about a week later. When I walked into my cube and saw a white envelope, I knew it was the photos. Quickly taking them out and staring at them for the longest time, my eyes would leak.

Before I surrendered to prison, I told my daughter she would be able to visit up to six hours. She said, "Six hours? What are we going to talk about for six hours?" I said, "I have no idea."

As it turned out, we never ran out of words. Some of our best conversations and time spent were on visiting day in prison.

My boys were on their own faith walk while I was detained. We naturally found ourselves submerged in scripture and discussing how to apply the messages heard at church in everyday life. Explaining parables always generated hours of discussion. We had our own church in the visiting room. The boys said they often felt rejuvenated after they left me, and I observed a renewed confidence and leadership they displayed. My imprisonment instilled qualities in them none of us could have imagined.

My family became regulars, and over time, the visiting families got to know one another. They were like neighbors. They waited long hours beginning at day break to ensure they would get a space in the visiting room. They found their own comfort and support with one another while sipping gas station coffee and exchanging phone numbers. Babies cried, different languages were spoken, teenagers watched, and little kids got restless. Grandparents stood quietly yet determined to see their loved one. They smiled and laughed but shared something else in common—a heavy ache.

As the clock ticked, we knew when it was near time to say our goodbyes. The guards would make an announcement as a reminder. My heart would start to beat strangely again, and my body would tighten. The expressions on our faces would change, and it was obvious why.

Trying to be nothing but grateful and loving, I would let my family know I was okay and not to worry. We would hug and cry and break into some needed comic relief. I would watch them exit as they waved goodbye and turned the corner.

Once the cleaning, sweeping, emptying garbage cans, restacking chairs, putting games away, and tables back in order were complete, we formed a long line to be checked out. We were not permitted to walk our visitors out, not like home. We always stayed behind.

Getting cleared to exit and return to the compound is different than getting cleared to enter visiting. Random strip searches make it like playing Russian Roulette. If the inmate before me had been in the room a long time, I knew she was probably getting stripped searched, so I would probably get passed over. I certainly got my fair share of strip searches.

As humiliating as the strip search was, I found it to be humorous at times. There was a wardrobe mirror attached to the back of a door, and the only time I saw myself naked was during a visiting strip search. And there'd I'd be—completely naked, peeking at my own body while some crazy guard watched me shake out my panties.

"Bend over, spread your cheeks, and cough." I felt sorry for the guard. Who would really want to look up another lady's anus? And then there was always the "creative guard" who would then ask me to turn around and do the same thing from the front. The first time I didn't understand. I said, "What do you mean from the front?" She said, "Lean back and spread your front." I responded, "Do I have to cough?"

The strip searches were so degrading, but it didn't matter, I focused on the fullness of knowing my family loved and supported me.

"Clear to leave."

Then I'd walk back up the hill to my other world, prison.

chapter eleven

Living a New Way of Thinking

Prison life was tolerable once I learned to change the way I looked at things. For example, instead of referring to the bleachers as bleachers, I referred to them as "the beach."

The summer in Alderson, West Virginia, can be hot as hell, especially on top of the mountain and closer to the sun. Women would exercise squatter rights for the most comfortable places on the beach. Trees canopied over some areas offering shade, while other areas were in full sun offering a sunburn and a tan. There was a place for everyone, if you were one of the first forty out of 1,200 women to get there. These were elementary-sized bleachers. Personally, I found the beach therapeutic for short periods of time, especially when I had space to stretch my legs and massage my back on the bench area behind me.

Obviously, we were not issued bikinis to wear. We all wore the same ugly, knee-length, gray, nylon shorts. The shorts couldn't be uglier or less flattering, but who cares when you are in prison? Who cares about shaving legs either? I was elated!

One day while Pinkey and I were at the beach working on our farmer's tans, we also were observing all the different kinds of women walking around the track. People-watching is continuous entertainment in prison. The beach had the most desirable view and was highly sought after. As Pinkey and I sat quietly in the VIP section, a new inmate approached us.

A lonesome lady in her forties strolled by us while trying to disguise her crying. It takes time to adjust, and she was only three months in. At first, she walked by. Then she paused and slowly turned toward us as if she wanted to say something or needed something. As I watched her, part of me hoped she would come over. She was probably still in shock, afraid and not sure who to talk to. Another part of me was cautious about inviting trouble to accompany us at the beach. Sometimes my heart gets me in trouble, and she could be one of the crazy ones.

I decided to wave and send her a warmhearted smile. Then Pinkey smiled and said, "C'mon over." (So much for being cautious.) Her crying stopped as she sat down with us on the beach. It was apparent she longed for someone to talk to. We all do, whether in prison or not. I don't think that ever changes. Pinkey and I were understanding and supportive, assuring her it would get better. We too remembered the same shattered feelings, feelings of disbelief, disparity, and utter exhaustion. The ladies who had arrived before me acted as my mentors and assured me that they too understood how it felt to arrive. "The prison sentence will get better; stay busy," they said.

They were right, although nobody told me I would have to learn to occupy my mind. I was used to working and managing clients and kids with time racing by. I struggled living in an unproductive environment until I met some good people. Yep, good people, you can find them anywhere, even in a prison. We encouraged her not to isolate herself and to find people who were fun to be around. Pinkey and I assured her she had just met the two best ones! The lonesome lady didn't feel quite as alone and finally laughed. We all laughed.

The compound was getting busier that afternoon. The weather was gorgeous, and even the women who rarely came out, came out to play that day. Getting out of those dark, depressing cubes and grabbing a change of scenery was good for the mind and soul.

As Pinkey and I continued to work on our tans, a lady in her fifties briskly walked directly towards us—yikes towards me! She stood directly in front of me and said, "Thank you!" I asked, "Thank you for what?" "For being so kind to me during visiting on Saturday," she answered.

Here's what happened: when the visiting area meets maximum capacity, the guard will ask the inmates who get regular visits if they would end their visits early for the others who don't get regular visits. I was with my family that day, and I had visits almost every weekend. When I heard the announcement, I felt it was only fair to let the guard know I would volunteer to end my visit if needed. I certainly don't have a halo over my head and didn't want to end my visit, but I couldn't help but imagine how crummy it would be for someone else who rarely got visits to end early. The guard said it was good to know, and she would let me know if I had to leave. My family stayed to the end though.

After visiting ended and all the visitors had left, the guards made us sit and wait to be released, about ninety minutes of sitting and waiting. Whether sitting, walking, or waiting, you're still serving time; it's just incredibly slow.

While we waited like zombies, I asked the lady next to me if she had a nice visit. She said it was her first visit ever, and it was wonderful. Then she said she panicked when she heard the room was at maximum capacity and the guards were asking people to leave. I told her I was grateful my family could visit me almost every weekend, and when I heard the announcement, I had volunteered to end our visit.

Visits are demonstrations of true love because they are inconvenient, tiresome, expensive, and often mournful. Yet I took mental photographs of the visits and could reflect on them when I needed motivation to get through the dark and unending days. Nobody should have to end their visits early.

Then another lady in her forties came over to tell me she had put me in her "God jar" and was praying for me. I had no earthly idea why, nor had I ever heard of a God jar. She said when she thinks about something or someone she wants to pray about, she writes it down on a scratch piece of paper and puts it in the jar. Before she prays, she empties the jar and looks at her pieces of papers to remind her of what to pray. I was touched to know someone was praying for me, but felt others needed her prayers too. I kindly asked her if she would remove me from the jar and put Pinkey in there; it would serve a better purpose. We got a good laugh out of that.

The last lady walked by, and Pinkey told me the lady was arrested for selling the same cemetery lots over and over. I said it didn't sound much different than the way the halfway house works. I heard the halfway house rents the same beds over and over. I guess once released, one can feel halfway dead!

It was another amusing afternoon at the beach on the bleachers. However, I considered changing the name to the Mount of Olives because it reminded me of Jesus spending time on the mount teaching and prophesying to his disciples. As we were packing up, I noticed a lady drinking coconut water and asked her if I could read the label. "Exotic flavor that sends your tongue on a tropical taste-cation," it said. I had to ask, "Is this a good drink for prisoners?"

The prison bleachers provided one of the most memorable beaches I've ever experienced. Pain and pleasure, completely opposite—we tend to avoid pain and seek pleasure. But in prison, I found myself running to those in pain because I derived a soulful pleasure in assuring them they weren't alone. Telling an inmate to find good women in prison sounded funny at the time Pinkey and I suggested it. There are good women and bad women in prison, just like there are bad women who are not in prison. Life is full of opposites!

I developed friendships with women, not based on what they did or what they didn't do, but on their hearts. Hearts whispered loudly. When the visiting room was at full capacity and the guards were looking for ladies to end visits early, I wasn't sure what to do. I really didn't want to volunteer and was hoping other ladies would, so I could stay with my family. Then I started making up reasons in my head why I shouldn't volunteer: "It's not fair to punish me just because I get visits every weekend. My family drove a long way too." Then I thought about my own family, if it had been their first visit or one of the rare times they were able to come. My family would be immensely let down. The thought of another family feeling deflated was beyond painful for me to swallow. You can hurt me, but don't touch my family. I wasn't trying to be kind; I was avoiding the pain in having another family suffer.

It was a morning
for walking slowly
and observing
God-given nature.
There was beauty
in the mountains
of West Virginia,
even though I was
standing in a prison.

chapter twelve

Sunday Morning Daydreams

Sunday mornings in prison were made for daydreaming. I would try to imagine what I would be doing if I were back in Charlotte.

I suppose two out of three of my kids would've gone to church, maybe out to lunch afterward, if I were buying. During the drive home or at the restaurant, we would talk about the message and what we each got from it and how it affected us. We would talk about how we would be able to apply what we learned to our everyday lives. You could feel your brain really thinking; sometimes it hurt. The best part was listening to how my boys were growing with a thirst for understanding God's word, something I did not have when I was growing up.

We certainly weren't perfect churchgoers, meaning every single Sunday. But for a while we consistently gathered on Sunday nights for dinner, a family church. Everybody would come ten to fifteen minutes apart bringing a little something, or Rocky would ask, "Oh, were we supposed to bring something?" It didn't matter. It was just nice to have everybody together. Even our dog, Boomer, sat on a chair at the table with us.

Throughout the house, it was easy to smell the pot roast cooking slowly. I didn't mind the extra work because it was worth it when the kids came in and would say, "Wow, something smells really good, Mom." We always kissed and hugged when we saw each other. And it wasn't just a kiss—it was a kiss on one cheek and kiss on the other cheek. In Italian, it's called *guancia a guancia*.

It wasn't easy getting everyone to sit down at the table at the same time. Somebody would be caught up watching a football game or on the phone, but eventually we would all sit down. Then the dreaded question I would ask: "Who wants to say the blessing?" Of course, they would put their heads down or volunteer one another. I would then jump in and say, "Okay, I'll do it." "Mom, please don't make it long. We want to eat while the food is still hot." I enjoyed saying the dinner prayer. The only reason I did it all the time was because I felt like I was the leader of the home, and I wanted my kids to be prepared when they had their own families. We always laughed because right after I said "amen" everybody would shout, "Let's eat!"

The boys would be salivating as they tossed the potatoes and green beans around the table, and of course, Alexi was proudly making jokes about it. We always had a delicious bottle of Cabernet wine or three, lots of laughter, and plenty of intriguing conversation. A perfect Sunday dinner.

As soon as the compound opened and we could go outside, I would stroll around the track holding my plastic mug of instant coffee. It was a morning for walking slowly and observing God-given nature. There was beauty in the mountains of West Virginia, even though I was standing in a prison.

As I walked around the track I could remember the happiness and love at my kitchen table. All I could envision was my family laughing. I missed them so much. I could see inside their mouths when they laughed. I could feel the clothes they wore—Rocky's plaid shirt, Alexi's brightly colored scarf she so often tied around her neck with her cute jewelry. And Zico had a special way of wearing a smile, one that magically lit up any room.

I purchased a small a.m. radio and headset from the commissary. There were a few Sunday morning church services I could find through the static, grateful to understand the message. Sunday morning in the mountains of West Virginia, I never had dreamed of that one!

Eventually the other ladies would be strolling out to the track with their plastic mugs of instant coffee, although we pretended it was from the Starbucks drive-through. As we gathered at the picnic table, I would inevitably share the message I heard on my fancy radio. These ladies weren't afraid to ask questions about the bible because they wanted an understanding. When none of us knew the answers, we would dig through the bible, seeking God's words. It was a lot more fun when nobody knew the answer.

Now don't think we didn't argue because everybody had their own viewpoint. But everybody participated in the conversation, whether they were speaking, reading, laughing, or crying. Nobody acted as if they knew it all, except the Senator. But we loved her anyway.

I think prison had a way of uncovering the worst of people so that the best of them could be exposed. Through the wrongdoings, drug addictions, or blatant crime, humility and vulnerability surfaced. The ladies at the picnic table were revealed according to who they really were.

Those Sunday mornings were nothing like Sunday dinner, but they were still very special. I think the departure of what I had helped me see all that I had. And sometimes realizing every moment of a Sunday night dinner should not to be taken for granted—that's a good thing.

The memories about my family and Sunday night dinners were not completely real. Although parts were very real, I only remembered the good ones. Fantasizing about my future Sundays with family could lead to nothing more than disillusionment. Nobody in my family would behave or do things the way I had in envisioned in my prison fantasy. It was my made-for-TV Hallmark movie, and they were my characters, yet they didn't know they had been cast. They hadn't even auditioned!

Instead when I returned, I returned to real life, a complicated life—hardly what I had expected. They too had endured experiences that affected them, although it had not been communicated until someone exploded, broadcasting misunderstanding and discontent. Piercing words flew out of mouths, eventually leading to exhaustion. Sometimes the tension would be so bad I wanted to go back to prison, but not really.

The Hallmark movie I had created turned into a drama series in which I did not know what my role was. Several members wanted the leading role, others had supporting roles, and some wanted no part of it. It took several nerve-racking months before my family ironed out the wrinkles that desperately needed pressing. We are a gathering of people, sharing one another's burdens. That's real church; that's a Sunday night dinner. As we each have our own distinct roles, we are still one body of a family. I'm forever grateful I was cast for my own part.

Sundays in prison were nothing like being at home, but they were still special.

chapter thirteen

The Club

During those scorching-hot, muggy days of summer, my friends and I would congregate in the air-conditioned library, which we called "Club Library" or the "Club" for short. We exercised our creative sides and placed a "reserved" sign on our table. It was preferred seating because it was next to the oscillating fan—total grandeur. When we flipped the sign over, it read "no corking fee." The other inmates looked at us like we were deranged. We may have been seriously out of our minds as we entertained our fantasy of sipping wine on the Amalfi Coast of Italy.

Danni, also known as "the Senator," was hostile and passionate about protecting the rights of other inmates. As a lesbian general contractor in her former life, she was often outraged about any violation she could find having to do with prison policy. Not that anyone really listened to her, but she sure did get fired up when she discovered loopholes within the system. Personally I loved her passion. And it certainly was fun crafting escape routes. (Just kidding.)

Although Pinkey was a Romanian fortune-teller, we called her the Professor. She didn't say much. She spent most of her time studying people. Her eyes had this unusual power to see through a person, ghoulish at times.

I was referred to as the Maya Angelou of the group. My passion was for peace, love, and happiness, which drove the Senator extra wacky. It became obvious to us that the next best thing, aside from the oscillating fan, was for us to produce and write our own sitcom.

The Professor was told to start jotting down her daily activities and to take detailed notes. She laughed and said she was the one who couldn't remember anything. We told her that was why we wanted her to write things down. (Full disclosure: if our sitcom is produced someday and the Professor has little input, it's because she forgot to take her notes.)

chapter fourteen

Gay for the Stay

When the Senator said she had a ten-year sentence, you could have knocked me over with a feather. Ten years? I can barely stand in line for ten minutes. She asked me the dreaded question, "How long are you in for?" Oh gosh, I really didn't want to answer her question. How could I tell another woman, who had a ten-year sentence, I only had twenty-one months? Ladies with long sentences took no mercy on those with less. "Don't cry on my shoulder. I've got ten years, while you suffer through your twenty-one months" kind of made me feel like I was no good, as if a longer sentence would have made me happy.

The Senator, convicted of a white-collar crime, was a general contractor from Pittsburg, in her forties, and gay. She was hysterically funny, opinionated, loudmouthed, intelligent, a ferocious fighter, and deaf in one ear. Her political distaste for the government, federal prison, guards, and the majority of inmates suited her well. The Senator had a rough and tumble attitude. For some oddball reason, I liked this no-nonsense lady from Pittsburgh, plus I knew there was a heart in there somewhere.

Since she was deaf in one ear, she learned to read lips. If I didn't want her to know what I was saying, I had to make sure I turned my head. That pissed her off! It was good entertainment, even though I'm not usually an instigator like my son Rocky.

Since the Senator was gay and in a women's prison for ten years, I thought there might be an upside (think about it). When I asked her if she would consider a relationship in prison, she almost fell off the four-foot aluminum bleachers. "Hell no! I'm not interested in a relationship in here." Then she asked me if I knew anyone on the outside I could introduce her to. "Seriously?" I said.

She then starting talking loud, louder, outside-voice loud, (she did that when she got excited, which was daily). "I'm gay, really gay, always gay. These women are not really gay!" Strangely, I felt they were imposters and felt honored to be friends with a "real" lesbian.

Consensual, same-sex prisoner relationships are common among both male and female inmates. It's not necessarily a reflection of their sexuality, but more a pragmatic counterbalance to loneliness. Many prisoners are simply "gay for the stay." Don't confuse gay with gay for the stay. I met women who were lesbians in their outside lives but not interested at all in relationships in prison. The ones who arrive to prison as heterosexual may get involved with women because they are seeking companionship and tenderness. The desire to be touched, embraced, and held becomes magnified when one realizes it's missing. Women either go without or choose gay for the stay.

I am not active in LGBT rights, but the common thread the Senator and I shared was the longing for human touch, holding a hand, giving and receiving a hug. For whatever the reason someone's sexual identity differs from yours, it doesn't mean they don't desire love. We all do.

Fortunately, my family visited often, and I could hug someone almost every week. Upon entering the visiting room—after being stripped search—the warmth of human contact began but only briefly. If I violated the rules, I could jeopardize the privilege of receiving visitors. There were times I would close my eyes only to forget I was in prison. I remember secretly trying to hold on to that feeling and would draw upon it to help me through the days ahead of me until the next visit.

Life outside the visiting room was different, a different standard. Technically, women are not supposed to hold hands, kiss, or display their affections. The operative word is "technically," but it happens, and everyone knows it. I never saw a guard do anything to stop it even when they knew it was happening. It was easier to turn a blind eye. I would look the other way as well because I felt uneasy passing two women kissing while they were trying to be "undercover." Awkward moment.

A few weeks prior to reporting to prison, a man asked me if I was permitted to have conjugal sex while cooped up. I couldn't help but ask him if there was anything else he wanted to know! He said that was about all he could think of. (Nice guy, right? Jerk!) The United States Bureau of Prisons does not allow conjugal visits for prisoners in federal custody.

Skin hunger is everywhere—in prison, in the bars, and look at Match.com. "Looking for someone to cuddle." "Looking for my last dance partner." "How will you author your next chapter?" Affectionate contact is necessary for a healthy life, and we suffer when we don't get enough! Be grateful every time someone reaches for your hand, kisses you, or—my favorite—gives you a big warm hug. Soak it up. Things change when it's missing.

I want to be a hug.

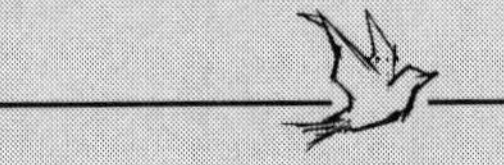

But when I finished
my last stitch,
simultaneously
exhaling and crying,
something inside me
knew these would be
the most special gifts
I had ever given.

chapter fifteen

Christmas Crocheting

The commissary was a small room where we shopped. The room contained items such as chips, cookies, instant coffee, dry milk, tuna fish, beans, candy, and peanut butter. There were also feminine products including shampoo, soap, hairbrushes, hair clips, mascara, and Preparation H. We had assigned days for shopping and were permitted to go one time per week. It was an adventure, like the once-a-year shoe sale at Nordstrom's.

I've never been separated from my family at Christmastime. Knowing this was inevitable, I began to imagine what it would be like for them as well. "It's going to be so obvious I'm not there; I am the life of the party!" "Oh, my God, will they remember me? Will they realize I'm not there?" "Where is Rudolph when you need him?" I did think about escaping.

I wanted to be positive about something. There must be benefits to being an inmate during Christmas. Well, here's one: you will not find hysterical holiday drivers—grouchy women, yes, but not driving. Here's another: you won't experience road rage or circle the parking lot painfully searching for a parking space. Oh, I'm on a roll now! You have no need for gift receipts—nothing is returnable in federal prison.

That Christmas I decided to crochet a scarf for my sister and daughter each and to knit caps for my two boys. Finally, after several frustrating months, I accumulated enough red, yellowish gold, black, and gray yarn, not exactly my taste for holiday colors. We had to choose based on what was in stock, no custom orders.

I also had to purchase the proper knitting needles along with a crochet hook for beginners. The prison commissary was not well stocked with these supplies, so I decided to plan ahead, in order to beat the urgent needs of 1,200 other frantic Christmas shoppers. Navigating for my knitting materials was not as simple as you might know it to be. It was a pain in the you know what.

Could you imagine how upset you would be if you made four trips to purchase yarn, knitting needles, and a crochet hook? Well, that is exactly what happened. Either the hook, needle, or yarn was not on the shelf but was expected the following day. The only problem with that was I was not able to return to the commissary for another seven days! By that time, the shelves were barren again. You would probably want to speak to the store manager, but I preferred to avoid the guards.

I hate to sew; this is total punishment. Honestly, I had no interest in knitting or crocheting, but I would be able to send them a one-of-a-kind memento, from prison. Their own personal souvenir! (Joy to the world.) Now I really felt like a prisoner.

Ladies took pride in their knitting projects and were extremely talented in creating some of the most beautiful items I've ever seen. Getting someone to teach me was easy, but I quickly learned they each had their own way to do things, the prison knitting way. I became confused as to which way to knit because each lady would tell me differently—"No, no, no, that's not right; that lady doesn't know," or "I've been knitting all my life; listen to me or don't ask for my help." Territorial knitting wars—this was stressing me.

After I found "my way" around the knit one and purl two, I had a purpose—man needs purpose even in prison—spending hours in Cube 44, propped up against the cinderblock wall, and knitting and crocheting my little fingers off. When I visualized Christmas morning,

I couldn't help but wipe the giddy smirk off my face. I imagined my diva daughter opening her package, pulling it out of the packing envelope, and saying, "Did mom make this? Does she expect me to wear this? This is oogly!"

But when I finished my last stitch, simultaneously exhaling and crying, something inside me knew these would be the most special gifts I had ever given—contributions from my heart, my effort, my dedication, and more than anything my love, motherly love.

I had to purchase special envelopes and the exact amount of postage to send these items home. This was no easy task either and took several trips to the "store." I wish we could have dropped packages into a metal bin leaving all our cares behind, but prison is not convenient.

After stuffing the scarves and caps into the envelopes, the last step was to get them "mail approved." There are specific days and times called "mail-out day." Typically, it's another long line without any guarantee the guard will show up to open the door. The next obstacle is whether your package will be approved for mail out. It was a victorious moment for me when the guard accepted my one-of-a-kind prison treasures. I couldn't wait for Christmas morning.

When the payphones were turned on, the line began to form on Christmas morning. The excitement of Christmas day was filled with a charge of joy and feelings of exhilaration, surprisingly found in a prison. Ladies were wishing one another a Merry Christmas, hugging, and laughing with tears of triumph.

It was my turn to punch in the phone number along with my eight-digit regulation number. It was ringing. The recording came on: "You have a call from a federal prisoner, Holly Pasut. Do you accept this call?" Heidi answered, "Holly!" Not knowing I was going to burst into tears, I said, "Merry Christmas, everyone!" I could hear everyone in the background, "Mom, Mom, Merry Christmas!" One by one they jumped on the phone to speak with me. Surprisingly shocked with my new knitting talents, Alexi thought I bought the scarf at the commissary!

The following week I received photos giving me a peek of what Christmas morning looked like for my family. Heidi and Alexi had their scarves on while the boys sported their knit caps. I could see a combination of strength, love, and sadness. If everything went as planned, I wouldn't get a Christmas photo the next year because I would be home. Many of us celebrate Christmas as a time of year to acknowledge the birth of Christ. We also are joined with our families and friends, surrounded by beautifully decorated trees, sparkling lights, mementos to exchange on Christmas morning, roasted turkey for dinner, cozy blankets, crackling fireplace, and movies. Towns are jam-packed with activities, parades, Santa Clauses, and Christmas wishes for the young and the old.

Even though my kids don't believe in Santa anymore, I still enjoy unpacking the Christmas tree, singing off key to Christmas music, and wrestling with the string of lights that were literally thrown into the box from the previous year. I still feel the same excitement I had when I was a little girl.

Is Christmas exciting because of the treasures under the tree, the bright lights in the windows, or the personal cards you receive in the mail? Is it the turkey dinner with family and friends or the snowman you build in the front yard? What's the purpose of hanging stockings anyway? People are festive and cheerful as they shout "Merry Christmas" to those they pass on the street—is this the meaning of Christmas?

For many, Christmas is a time of sorrow, too, not having enough money to fill Christmas stockings for their children or loved ones. Savoring the taste of a roasted turkey is only a wish and not a reality. Many are saddened when they cannot be with the ones they love. I understood what this felt like.

Today, I remember Christmas as symbolic of generosity, rather than marshmallow fluff or red scarves. Big-heartedness is a quality like honesty and patience. Can I have enough goodness?

Giving gifts and putting others before myself is also free giving. But charity is about more than cash and stuff. Kindness is about forgiving and being gentle to people; that's the heart of spirit. Helping others, giving them credit for doing something nice, a compliment—that too shows high-mindedness. Wouldn't Christmas and the whole world be a more pleasant place to live if people showed generosity? It's so easy and doesn't require prison or meeting postage requirements.

My first Christmas home, I had a variety of feelings and one sorrow. I thought about the ladies in prison on Christmas morning—the lines at the payphone, while some had no one to call.

During Christmas, the commissary supplies a few holiday yummies and sweet treats to purchase. Supply is low, and price is high, but when it comes to the marshmallow fluff, women want it. The fluff comes in a huge plastic container, and they scoop spoonfuls into their mouths. Marshmallow fluff had more followers than Beyoncé.

One day around Christmas back in prison, my "bunkie" (roommate) was anxiously awaiting her family to send her extra money, so she could buy the famous marshmallow fluff. When I got home one evening—did I say home? It wasn't home. I meant when I walked into Cube 44, she was wallowing, sobbing, seriously lying on the concrete floor anguishing with despair. I thought something horrible had happened. Not knowing what to do, I asked, "Are you okay?" I know that was a stupid question. Obviously, she wasn't okay. What do you do in these kinds of situations? Then she said, "I'm so sad; all I wanted was some marshmallow fluff for Christmas."

Giving impulsive and expensive stuff of worldly values are only feeding the appetites of those who love the world. Perhaps it wasn't the inability to purchase marshmallow fluff, but the extreme disappointment in lack of thoughtfulness and kindness from her family. She felt forgotten.

While living in the halfway house, we were required to meet weekly for "group." I listened to a gentleman who was dispirited about his niece. He was not a man with an abundance of disposable income; however, in an effort to form a loving relationship with her, he bought her a pair of stylish new boots. A few days later she was highly disrespectful toward him, as if his giving gesture in purchasing the boots was long forgotten.

I know you cannot buy someone else's love. But when the recipient loves the gift more than the giver, I think we have a problem. Don't you think? But I (and probably you) do it anyway because it's Christmas for goodness sake.

While I give, I choose to remember that Jesus is still the reason for the season. Yes, Jesus is even better than Santa Claus!

chapter sixteen

Compassionate Payphones

There's nothing sexy about a payphone. They are bulky, sticky, and dirty, and you never know if they're going to operate correctly. You may not be old enough to remember payphones. Back in the day you could spot them on the side of the road or at the corner gas station, and my favorite was the phone booth. They're not just for Superman. If you were gymnastically inclined, you could try squeezing two people in a phone booth. Hopefully, nobody had an unpleasant odor of the breath! (Are you picking up what I'm laying down?)

I remember when I didn't lose my phone. There was a time when a phone knew its place. The phones in federal prison were exactly where you expected them to be. There was never a need to search the prison looking for the payphone. A row of payphones hung on the wall with a wooden bench in front of them.

These were special payphones. They didn't accept coins. I had to punch in a set of numbers that took me thirty-seven days to memorize. I felt somewhat inferior; I had to keep my numbers on a tiny piece of scratch paper because I couldn't remember them. It wasn't difficult to notice the amazing speed with which the younger women could punch their numbers into the phone—phone-punching Olympians.

The phones were only open during specific times of the day, and when women began forming the line, you knew the phones would be turned on soon. The anticipation of hearing my family's voices on the other end made waiting in line worthwhile.

There were times I would run out of money or out of minutes and would not be able to speak to my family for a few weeks. But sadly, there were many women who never left their bunks to stand in the phone line. They had no one to call. I felt grateful to be one of those standing in the line.

The funniest conversations were when bilingual women were speaking Spanish. The conversations began in the normal audible range, then got a bit louder, increasingly louder to unbelievably louder, then fast, to faster, then exceedingly fast, then suddenly a recognizable word: "Sh—!" They swore in English.

One time my son said he couldn't hear me, but he could hear everybody else. I asked, "Whose conversation are you listening to—the lady next to me screaming at her boyfriend or the young mother talking baby talk to her child?"

As unnerving as the payphone conversations were, the payphone area was a place for women to communicate and observe one another. Whether a woman is in prison or not, you will hear her talking sweetly to her child, you will hear her self-doubt with her boyfriend or spouse, you will hear her congratulating her children for their accomplishments, and you might join her to sing happy birthday to someone special.

Some conversations didn't go unnoticed. Those were times when a woman bit her lower lip or dropped her head into her hand or perhaps she would slide down the wall to the floor—those were the bad ones. However, as soon as she hung up the phone, another woman would sit next to her, hold her, rock her, and let her cry.

If ever there was a display of compassion between different ethnicities, races, religions, and gender identifications, it was at the payphones. Maybe we need to sprinkle a few payphones around town.

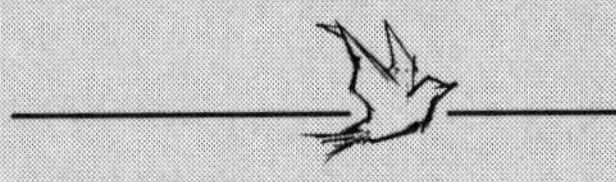

Please say a quiet
prayer for those who
are incarcerated,
without judging their
lives or choices. Truly,
you don't know anything
about them. Let them
not forget how to smile
today or tomorrow.

chapter seventeen

The Ones Left Behind

Have you heard it said, "You have to be a friend to have friends"? Happily for me, I had many friends before I went to federal prison. My best friends wrote me often and sent me books, and two of my very best friends mailed me a personalized monthly newsletter, which was hysterical. Prayer warriors were revealed as they encouraged me and assured me I had not been forgotten.

After I "checked in"—okay, surrendered—was the first time I felt as if I had no friends; I was living with strangers in prison (hardly a dream come true) and feeling as if I had tumbled down a rabbit's hole; and I was the only one at the bottom.

My vision became blurry, my environment was spinning, and my eyes dampened (we call that sweaty eyeballs)—okay, tears, lots of tears. My first few weeks, I was referred to as "that lady," the one with unfathomable sobbing. I did cry easily, still do. I'm working on getting a grip. (Okay, not really.)

Alderson Federal Prison Camp houses about 1,200 women. (Notice I didn't say "ladies." There's a reason. Just go with it.) It's easy to see the same faces repeatedly, followed by more meaningless conversations. For instance, we wouldn't say, "I like your shoes"—duh, we all had the same pair—or "Where did you get those hideous pants?" The elastic waistbands were not necessarily attractive, but offered *ease from constraint.*

There is a rule in prison: do not ask why someone is in prison or "how long will you be locked up?" Most of us were warned not to ask those questions. So, I was shocked the first time I was approached and someone asked me about my sentence. Women like to talk, women are nosy, and women compare sentences. It became very common to ask, "Why are you here?" Next—how long? Instantaneous bonding. Bam!

Once the gory details of a case were exposed, it became something to talk about and at times endlessly. I knew more about others' cases than my own. Prison can also be a land of fantasy, meaning you can be anyone you want to be in prison. Who would know? Who would really care? I have no earthly idea if what I was told was true, false, inflated, exaggerated, or overestimated.

Another inmate with unimaginable character became one of my walking buddies. She claimed to be a former mayor, runway model (or run-away model), firefighter, real estate investor, and competitive barrel rider, and was married to a world-class drug lord who was serving a ten-year sentence and with whom she shared a phenomenal sex life. And did she also say professional kick boxer? I can't keep it all straight. She was a mass of strange happenings, but oh so intriguing! I felt like such a bore in comparison. Welcome to "will the real offender please stand up?"

The picnic table was our place of bonding. You have wine and Bunco; we had picnic tables—sitting hour after hour, day after day, week after week, month after month, year after year. That's a lot of wine and Bunco.

A wealth of information could be observed while sitting at a picnic table, and through that came a familiarity and a bond—understanding a variety of personalities, enjoying the different senses of humor, examining good and bad motives, and knowing some ladies were encouragers while others needed constant encouragement. It was not uncommon to share tears and memories of family, including current family problems. We tried to keep up with the news, yet by the time we got the newspapers, it was old news. We debated it anyway. Interruptions in our daily prison life became our current news. Anything unexpected made the headlines, such as laundry changes or if the commissary would be selling marshmallow fluff, or if new yarn colors arrived.

The daily menu was always a hot topic, especially on chicken day. Let the trades begin—I'll give you my chicken for your apple pie. We exposed our perhaps unrealistic dreams and some of our worst nightmares and feelings of remorse. Regrets were widespread and usually revealed pent-up emotions. We would cry, hug each other, or sometimes just sit there with our chins in our hands. Families were a trigger for many people because not everyone had a family. Many women were disowned. They likely stole, lied, and used their friends and family until they had no more. Talking about kids could be either funny or about problems their kids were having at home. If the kids were having problems, it became escalated for the mother while incarcerated. As parents, we could do nothing. It was like watching a child drown while unable to throw them a lifeline. Some women experienced weddings, babies being born, and unfortunately, family funerals. Ladies celebrated the weddings and babies being born, but the deaths took a great toll. You might find a woman lying in her bunk for a few days, burying her face in the pillow, and unable to eat. We would give support by a light touch on her back as we passed by. At least she knew there were people around her who cared.

Gardening tips, fashion styles, favorite recipes, favorite husbands—did I say favorite husbands? I've been married more than once, and I have a favorite—most memorable vacay places, skin care secrets—few topics were off limits. We spent our time singing old hit songs, learning about different religions, discussing origins of the many different languages, races, and cultures around us, teaching English or math, celebrating achievements, losing weight, transforming, walking, praying, or staring at the mountains in silent company. Even though we had our own unique stories, we had something very much in common—prison, an unspoken understanding, an awareness of sadness and loss. No words required.

As a felon, I am not permitted to contact other felons. It's the law. Before leaving, I made it clear to those friends I left behind not to expect a letter, post card, or anything. Our friendships lasted while we experienced prison, but now they're only in hearts and memories.

After prison, I rejoiced in reuniting and reengaging with my prayer warriors, lasting friends. But there is something about spending time with strangers at a picnic table in the prison yard.

Please say a quiet prayer for those who are incarcerated, without judging their lives or choices. Truly, you don't know anything about them. Let them not forget how to smile today or tomorrow. (And, yes, I have sweaty eyeballs.)

chapter eighteen

Mail Call and the Pink Chain

In my daily life, days go by before I go to my mailbox. Why rush to open bills? Prison mail, however, was like celebrating Christmas morning Monday through Friday with letters and packages delivered in a pick-up truck instead of a sleigh. When the bags were lifted from the back of the truck, the heavier the better.

The guard would come through the door and yell, "MAIL CALL," and we would fly off the bunks and walk as fast as possible to the horseshoe. The horseshoe, which was shaped like a horseshoe (so original), was located at the front of the range. It was the designated place we lined up to check in and out of the range. We also gathered there for announcements, and it was the only place guards would sit. (I have to add, it was the only place where there was a padded chair, on which inmates were not permitted to sit. I was tempted to try to sit for only a minute, especially when my back was aching from all the standing. Thankfully, it was a passing temptation.) We would gather around the horseshoe hoping to hear our names called. "Gonzalez. Butler. Greenberg. McLaughlin

… McLaughlin? Where's McLaughlin? If you were not present to receive your mail, you might catch the evening mail call around 9:30 p.m. or the next day. But who knew?

I was one of the more fortunate ones because I received mail almost daily. My daughter made sure of that. You see, before I arrived at Alderson, I decided to be part of my own rescue. I purchased brightly colored index cards and wrote a scripture or question or some thought-provoking statement on approximately 365 cards. I asked my daughter, Alexi, to mail a card to me every day, and she did. As interesting as the cards were, I thought of my daughter every time I opened the envelope. The cards were intended to take my mind out of prison and give me something to dream about. Instead, I would study her handwriting on the outside of the envelope and wonder where she mailed them from. Touching something she had touched with her soft, skinny, little fingers, I felt close to her.

Sometimes I would take the card to my friends on the compound, and we would find ourselves in meaningful conversations. At least it took our minds out of the confined area we lived in. It gave us hope and integrity.

Sadly, some ladies never got off their bunks during mail call. Of course, I was curious as to why. I opened my big mouth one day and asked one lady I felt comfortable with. She said no one in her family had anything to do with her anymore. She had burnt every bridge she had with every friend and family member.

Laura was a drug dealer and addict. She stole money from everyone she knew along with stealing things from other people's cars and houses to support her addiction. She said she didn't blame everyone for cutting her off. She knew what she did was wrong but because of the drugs couldn't help becoming someone she didn't want to be.

Many of the ladies arrested for drugs were grateful to be clean and off the streets. They concluded that had they not been locked up, they would probably be dead. Prison saved them, and the thought of a new life someday was scary and exciting for some of them.

One day a lady who never got mail had her name called. Of course, she was in her cube because she didn't expect to hear her name. So when it was called, I became ecstatic for her and walked as fast as permitted down the hall to let her know. "Weber, the guard called your name. You have mail!"

She reacted like a long-tailed cat in a room full of rocking chairs. She flew off her bunk and anxiously speed walked to the horseshoe in hopes of retrieving it. It was too late. The guard had finished and walked away while telling her to make sure she was present for the evening call.

By the time ladies received newspapers—the *New York Times*, *Miami Herald*, or *Washington Post*—the news was old. But it was still wonderful to sift through the paper reading featured articles and book reviews and glimpses of the latest fashions. We pretended we were going shopping and picked out restaurants with rave reviews.

The timing of the mail call was tricky. After the mail had been handed out, we lined up for dinner, leaving little time to read our letters. I liked to savor my letters, so I would hide them under my pillow and come back after dinner to sit down, read, laugh, or cry quietly and without rushing.

Sometimes the letters were so beautiful, well written, and heartfelt, I couldn't resist sharing with some of my friends. Over time many of us felt close to one another's children just from sharing stories and letters about them. We knew about birthdays, graduations, girlfriends, boyfriends, spelling bees, and who hit a home run. We also knew about broken arms, failing the test, dropping out of school, getting arrested, and diagnosed with depression and cancer.

Mail call produced laughter, tears of joy, and unfortunately tears of great sadness—love letters, hate letters, "I want a divorce" letters, or worst of them all, a "someone died" letter. Mail call could be double jeopardy; you never knew.

Alexi sent me monthly affirmations on the cutest, most cheerful looking envelopes and cards. As soon as I saw the happy envelope, I knew it was her. With that lick of the envelope and drop into the mailbox, my daughter was thinking of me.

We were permitted to tape things inside our locker doors. (You have a dresser or closet; I had a metal locker. You have a handle or door knob; I had a lock.) As long as I could remember the combination, I could open it.

I wanted to tape Alexi's affirmations inside the locker, but I didn't have tape. My resourceful bunkie showed me how to use the leftover pieces on a sheet of stamps—those little extra strips along the edges. Prison had a way of stretching the imagination.

Not only did inmates get creative; my friends on the outside did as well. Kelly, who was a paralegal, would scoop up the old magazines from the office—*Family Circle*, *Better Homes and Gardens*, non-controversial types—and mail them to me. An accountant friend, Leslie, sent me a soft-back, leather-bound journal. The smell of the leather reminded me of a horse saddle or a new pair of Italian shoes. I walked around sniffing my new journal for days. I wasn't the only one obsessed with this divine scent. Leather has a way of combining every good and pleasurable experience into one sniff. Many women couldn't wait to get their noses on my new gift. I still remember the smell today.

I will never forget the day while standing at mail call, I spotted a letter with red lipstick kisses imprinted on every inch of the envelope. Immediately I thought of Laura, a beautiful friend who would take great measures to write to me weekly. She had a profound way of expressing her heart with her hand. I believe she had suffered greatly from her own pains. Although hers was different from mine, she understood pain. Pain is pain.

She would make a cup of herbal tea with honey, light her candle, and begin pouring out what was buried in her soul, filling the pages up from side to side, front and back. She left very little spacing between the lines. Seriously, she filled every blank space of her stationery.

Laura liked to wear bright colored lipstick and wouldn't go anywhere without her "lips on." Once the envelope was licked closed, Laura would seal it with a red kiss. Literally!

The first time I got one of her letters, I thought it was loving. Then came another one and another one. A red-lipstick-covered envelope has its own mystery, but between the guards, inmates, and me, we couldn't help but raise our eyebrows. We eventually stopped questioning the kisses—just accepted and smiled.

I appreciated and treasured the unique cards from Elizabeth along with the uplifting and encouraging books from Maggie. The anonymous letters of support renewed my faith in people. Love does exist. Mail call was a memorable event for me. It was like a huge hug, reassuring me I had not been forgotten.

My favorite and longest-lasting series of mail came from my sister, Heidi. My expected release date had fallen through, and I had no idea when I would be released. Basically, I was eligible to leave but had to wait until there was space at the halfway house in Charlotte, North Carolina. The only thing I could do was wait, pray, and listen for the red phone.

The happiest phone call I ever made was calling my sister with my official release date. She could barely understand what I was saying. I was crying, whispering, and gasping for breath all at the same time.

Heidi was screaming on the other end, "Holly, are you okay? What's going on? I can't understand you! Holly? Holly!"

I finally got ahold of myself. "Heidi, I have a date. I'm coming home."

Afterward, I received an envelope and didn't understand what I found inside. It was pink, taped, folded pieces of paper. I saw typing on each piece and numbers. I gently lifted the contents from the envelope and wondered why Heidi sent me shredded paper. Extremely confused yet enthusiastic to figure it out, I started shaping the pieces based on the zigzag of each folded piece. It was a chain!

Each piece in the chain had a descending number counting down to my release date and inside had something to read. Many of the quotes on the chain were hysterical. Heidi is a successful professional but not without painstaking long hours. Yet we both embraced making each other laugh. My pink chain was my sister's alter ego. "If it requires putting on lipstick, doing my hair, or wearing a bra, it's not happening today" or "Sometimes I think, 'Screw this ... I'll just be a striper.' Then I remember I'm fat ... and can't dance." I would stuff little pieces of the pink chain in my pockets and peek at them all day long—giggle out loud! The chain slowly got smaller and smaller before my very eyes. I was really going home.

Unfortunately, release delays were not rare. I watched many women eager to return to their homes and family, only to hear they would have to be rescheduled for a later time. My side bunkie had the same misfortune with a three-month setback. Talk about disheartened. She was literally in the pits. It was hard to watch because she was typically cheerful and free spirited. She deflated.

How could I help this lady out of her hole? Hmmm ... maybe I could pay it forward to her! Since I didn't have construction paper, I used my notebook paper and decorated one side of each paper slip with colorful stripes, polka dots, or some combination. On the other side, I wrote funny things she could relate to that would either make her think or laugh. Ugh, her chain looked long. But once done and numbered in descending order, I anonymously and strategically placed it under her pillow.

Her chain was a hit. We all witnessed her free spirit lifting day after day. I would even hear her on the compound saying, "I got to go pull my chain today!"

Heidi was, and is, a very busy real estate agent, and making a pink chain for her put-away sister was probably not on her personal bucket list. But it had a lasting impact for ladies who get set back at Alderson Federal Prison Camp. Before I left, I asked my bunkie to keep it going—to make a chain for anyone else getting delayed and so on and so on and so on.

It all started at mail call.

section three

Going Home

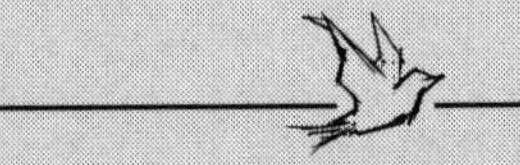

Whom could I trust in
prison? Even though
I met ladies whom I
considered friends,
I chose to hold a
perfect tension of
knowing them and
not knowing them.

chapter nineteen

Trust

Trusting people was never an issue for me. I trusted most everyone and quite easily. I eventually learned I was too trusting. Prison cured me of trusting anyone.

Prison was scary at first, and I wanted a friend, anyone, someone. I wanted to find a person I could get to know, get close to, someone with whom I could share stories. I found a handful of women I felt comfortable around—typical white-collar folk, educated, mature, and did I say opinionated?

Although in prison, you can be whoever you want to be. An uneducated woman could claim to be a professor, the drug lord could be a pharmacist, and the unloved could be a family therapist. Sometimes I was the future ex-wife of Donald Trump, and my friend was a princess.

Time has a way of revealing the character of people. In a way, that is a great thing. But in prison, time is not something one is hoping for more of. Similar to the outside world, however, at some point you meet someone, and a friendship is developed.

In prison I spent hours, days, weeks, and months sitting on picnic tables (if only picnic tables could talk). My friends and I would turn pages of old newspapers or flip through mindless magazines together. We'd crochet, cry, laugh at stupid things, and compare family drama together. We'd stand next to each other in slow moving lines, sit together during meals, and eat fish that wasn't for human consumption. We would make "appointments" to meet one another in places such as the library or chapel. It was the life and how friendships were formed in prison.

I would find myself looking for that person when I went outside on the compound and experienced a feeling of relief and happiness when I found them. After a period of time, we found ourselves comfortable sitting together, without words, because we understood the unspoken language of silence, patience, hope, faith, and pain. We were simply there for one another.

It's not uncommon for ladies to part while in prison over different beliefs, rumors, behaviors, change of character, or maybe an increase of awareness and wisdom. It all happens in prison; it happened to me. Suddenly a friend turned on me for reasons I don't know, may never know. I learned to just accept and keep moving. Inevitably and sadly friends are always separated. One gets released, and one is left behind, and then it starts over again.

Whom could I trust in prison? Even though I met ladies whom I considered friends, I chose to hold a perfect tension of knowing them and not knowing them. I couldn't be 100 percent sure of any inmate. An inmate is someone confined to an institution, hospital, or prison. Does that sound trustworthy?

Could it be a staff member? There was a definite line between the staff and an inmate. The staff was paid not to trust inmates. My personal experience confirmed that.

Pills were distributed by a nurse, so I had to line up outside in what was referred to as "pill line." I had to be in pill line twice a day, and it was drilled into us to be on time, or staff could refuse to give you medicine. I didn't want to be sick, especially in prison.

One afternoon, I couldn't get to the pill line on time because I had hair color all over my head. Prison had a cosmetology school, and I gratefully and with much enthusiasm had my grays covered whenever I could get an appointment. The cosmetology school was offered to inmates who qualified. (Not everyone qualified. Is that discrimination?) I believe you had to have been sentenced a minimum of five years and, thankfully, I did not qualify.

It was a snowy, icy, rainy day, and already dark at 2 p.m. in the afternoon, and it was time for pill line. Yikes! I didn't know what to do. I was in a West Virginia cosmetology school in a federal prison with the slowest student, slopping wet hair color all over me, which made me feel chilly and shivery. Imagining a warm cappuccino or a glass of Merlot like at the salons I went to at home only depressed me. On the upside, it was free, and tipping was not permitted. It was a bargain, after all. I told the lady-guard-teacher person I needed to go to pill line, but she said she would call and let them know my situation. I was told to go to health services (HSU) after my hair was completed, so I did.

Once I got to HSU, they refused to administer my medicine. *Say whuuut?* Now here comes the sticky-icky part. When I tried to explain what happened to the HSU staff, they did not believe me. I told them the lady at cosmetology told me she called to let them know I was delayed. They said nobody called to tell them about my extended time at the spa. Hmmm, somebody was not being truthful. Would you believe the inmate?

I was warned upon my arrival to prison never to challenge the staff. Whoever holds the keys holds the power. I was mortified, shocked, and outraged, but there was nothing I could do about it. Sadly, I eliminated staff members as people I could trust, which included guards, nurses, doctors, and counselors (anyone with keys).

Whom did I trust in prison? Is trust based on reliability, support, assistance? Is it based on having someone who believes in me? Was it the person who sent me mail and put money "on my books" so that I could purchase toothpaste? Was it the people who visited me regularly? Was it the people who said they loved me? Was it family?

My family did all those things, but were there times when we had tension, conflicting attitudes, or disagreements? Truthfully, yes. At times, I felt as if I were living on the edge of trust where I got parts of a story, different stories, or maybe half truths. But the underlying trust was always there. I trusted my family. We battled through prison together, one step, one day, one letter at a time.

Cube 44 became more than a place I slept. It became my "inner room." It was a place I could hide, especially at 5 a.m. while everyone else was asleep, propping myself up on my cozy-lumpy bed and leaning against the cold pink cinder-block wall. My pillow was as thin as a piece of paper, so I would roll up my partially made crochet blanket and mush it nicely behind me against the concrete wall. The darkness was my peace, and my book light was my most special necessity. I would get lost in my reading.

My favorite book was the bible and anything having to do with spiritual learning, intuition, understanding the true self, acknowledging the false self, wisdom, seeing as the mystics see, Christianity, Hinduism, Buddhism, Judaism, Kabbalah for beginners (Kabbalah is not what I thought, nor am I ready for that), and contemplative prayer. I devoured page after page, over and over, with my mind, imagination, memory, and tears, even happy tears. My highlighter was always nearby along with my pen and spiral notebook. Reading and journaling for ninety minutes every morning in prison was my personal escape.

I found my best friend in Cube 44. My friend was always awake when I wanted to talk and never left a voicemail or said, "Come back later when I have time." My friend allowed me to pour my heart out, and even at times I couldn't find the right words, my friend would say, "Don't be afraid. It's okay." Sometimes I would get mad at my friend, but I always knew my friend wouldn't abandon me, because my friend was patient, strong, and understanding. Even though I couldn't understand my friend all the time, I knew it was for my own good. This friend had a way of knowing my sadness too, always giving me assurance it was a part of the journey while goodness would be revealed. My friend only asked me to have faith. My friend made me feel deeply comfortable, safe, and loved. I would wake up every morning and say, "What's happening, best friend?" I think my friend would laugh. We giggled quietly together. I was completely in love with my friend.

My friend helped me to lay down my anger, bitterness, and cynical thoughts about our government and justice system. Living in my past only increased my pain while decreasing my focus and elevating my blood pressure. My friend encouraged me to surrender all of it. I think my friend knew it would take me time, and strangely time was on my side. My friend said if I was willing to stop holding on to it, it could be lifted off me.

The more time I spent with my friend, I found a true joy dwelling inside of me despite my circumstances. Even though I felt broken inside, lost, and hanging in a gap, I had a sense of peace and a thirst to have more of my friend.

I started to see things differently. My lens became a different color. It broadened and expanded. It felt right. My friend has this unique read on me, and once I started reaching for my friend, I think my friend began to raise me the rest of the way out of my own personal prison. I wanted whatever my friend wanted for me. I knew it would be better than anything I could imagine.

Even though I may never understand my friend's ways, I have come to accept my friend's strange ways without question. I think my friend is a pretty cool dude. I respect and love my special friend.

Prison was a place of revealing and awakening. My friend is the one I came to rely on and trust. My friend was always there, so I was never truly alone. I don't want to return to prison (as an inmate anyway), but when I look back, I'm grateful for the trip.

My friend was with me when I arrived in prison (timing is important to my friend), we lived together in Cube 44, we sat, we talked and walked daily, and together we tried to eat fish on Friday that was utterly disgusting. My friend taught me that nobody goes untouched by adversity and about how to endure my trials. When it was time for my release, my friend said, "C'mon, Holly, we're out of here. Let's go together."

My friend is with me today, all day and every day, forever. He developed me during my descent into hell and escorted me to the other side, through his grace and goodness. Oh, his name is God. I thought you knew!

Babbling about the
dream is not the
blueprint. Analyzing the
dream may be limiting
to the possibilities of
an unexpected success.

chapter twenty

Dreams

My morning routine back in prison was to wake up at 5 a.m. and immediately put the lanyard with my ID badge around my neck, slip my feet into my rubber slides (never touch the concrete floor), open my locker, and grab my toothbrush, toothpaste, and plastic mug with instant coffee and dried milk that I prepared the night before. First stop: the bathroom to wash my face and brush my teeth. Next stop: the microwave room to get hot water. Quickly walk back to Cube 44 and get back into bed before the guard does rounds at 5:15 a.m. Prop up against the cold cement block wall, turn on my book light, put on my glasses, and reach for my journal and pen to read and write for a little while. Then get dressed, make my bed, and sweep the room in time to walk to breakfast at 6:30 a.m. After breakfast, stand in the pill-line, get books, go to class, go to lunch, go to work, get back in pill line, go to mail call, go to dinner, take joy in free time, shower, and go to bed. Repeat.

Every day was the same day. Even the menu stayed the same. Thursday was always chicken day, and ladies would wake up and say, "Today is chicken day!"

Do you live each day like the movie *Groundhog Day* where every day is the same—are you programmed to get up, go to work, go to the gym, go home, eat dinner, watch TV, and then go to bed? Tomorrow you do it all over again? Scheduled, strictly organized, controlled, and stagnating? (Have you created your own personal prison?)

Time in prison slowly weakens the brain if you are not careful. Finding meaningful activity became a priority for me. At the beginning of boredom came fear of becoming stupid. I hoped someone would escape just for excitement. (Someone did!) I seldom dreamed a fire drill at 3 a.m. in the pouring rain would be a pleasant change of scenery, but it was! When gay couples had lovers' quarrels, the compound went into "enquiring minds want to know" mode! We longed for any change in the routine, good or bad.

Not even a random breathalyzer test first thing in the morning was beyond my idea of entertaining. One time I walked into CDR and cheerfully said good morning to the table of guards who sat together every morning. Apparently, I was overly joyful, so they beckoned me to their table. "Why are you so happy, Pasut? Blow in the breathalyzer." Walking away, I thought to myself, "Sure, I always have a double vodka first thing in the morning, especially in prison."

With a passion to see the world differently, I decided to expand toward my dreams, whatever they were. One of my favorite quotes by Henry David Thoreau: "I learned this, at least, by my experiment: that if one advances confidently in the direction of his dreams, and endeavors to live the life which he has imagined, he will meet with a success unexpected in common hours."

If your dream makes you feel alive, Thoreau says, you will meet an unexpected success! I believe God has something greater planned than you or I can ever imagine. But (don't you hate sentences that begin with a but?) you must discover a dream.

I gave myself permission and encouraged myself to think if I could do anything or create a new life, what would it look like? It was something I had never thought about. How big do I go? What's too big? Is there such a thing? How do I know what I really want? Prison was a safe place to begin dreaming.

I heard the quality of life is determined by the questions we ask of ourselves. So I began asking myself questions I had never given thought to, navigating toward my own dream.

Discovering my dream was not as easy as I thought it would be. What were my longings and discontents trying to tell me? What did I want more of or less of? Could it really happen? Why did I doubt myself? What would my perfect day look like?

Visualizing my perfect day—who I was with, what I read, what kind of food I ate, the décor of my new office—I could feel the sun on my shoulders when I walked outside, the smell of the scented candles in the morning, the view of nature from my window with family close by. Life was good. I envisioned every aspect of the areas of my life, including health, relationships, profession or vocation, time, and financial freedom.

Would my dream give me more life? Would my dream align with my core values? Would my dream cause me to grow? Would my dream require a higher power, greater than my intellect? Would my dream bring a greater good or goodness for others?

At one time, I thought it would be fun to be an activity director on a cruise ship, traveling the seas, meeting new people, relishing yummy food and nightlife. I would bring energy and enthusiasm, perfect for this kind of position, yet at the same time I would be miserable. Family is an important part of my life, and knowing this, I crossed the idea off my list because it didn't align with my core values.

Shortly after I was released, I wanted to know more about creating dreams and living an intentional life. Most of my adult life I never dreamed. I was happily preoccupied raising my family, managing clients, and "spurring the economy" (that's code for shopping).

Attending a premier training center for transformational coaching at The Life Mastery Institute, I graduated as a Certified Dream Builder Coach. While learning to assist others in navigating their own personal dreams, I learned how to discover my own.

Babbling about the dream is not the blueprint. Analyzing the dream may be limiting to the possibilities of an unexpected success. Committing myself to move toward the dream was a step in my personal transformation. My options (and yours):

1. Do nothing and live the life I am living.
2. Come to the realization and acceptance that my dream is my dream. I own it; therefore, I must self-initiate. I cannot expect others to make my dream come true.
3. Seek an understanding, and don't be afraid to pause and say, "Hmmm, what is it I am saying?"

After returning home to a life of unfamiliarity, I took an opportunity to draw a blueprint of what I wanted out of life. But I still didn't know; I only knew I could not be a real estate agent anymore. The past life, which I knew and was successful in, was over.

Another one of my favorite quotes (unfortunately, I do not know who said it) is, "Some people live ninety years; other people live one year ninety times."

I know which one I choose.

chapter twenty-one

Sipping Coffee with God

God and I hang out every morning, typically before dawn. While it is dark, still, and silent outside other than a few birdies chirping, it's a tranquil time of the day. We sip our coffee, we laugh, and I ask questions and shed a few tears. (If you know me, you know I am a weeping woman.) God is attentive, exceedingly wise, and I suspect he has a sense of humor.

These intimate conversations and prayers are held in a specific room in my tiny townhouse. It's the other bedroom; I only have two. Traditional people might deem the spare room as their guest room. My guest room is my sanctuary and has no bed. It is decorated with beautiful pictures, well-read books, family photos, strings of happy lights, and scented candles. The soft yellow chaise, my "prayer chair," is angled under the standing lamp with a magnificent feather dangling from under the lampshade. Strategically placed next to my chaise is my favorite bamboo tray table with journals, books, and several bibles. It's not about the coffee; it's my morning ritual.

One morning I stopped asking for direction because I knew God already knew what I wanted. God knows everything I aspire to, so why do I continually ask? Besides, I felt like I was bugging him, the way my kids bugged me when they were younger. (They bugged me relentlessly and then I would give in. Hmmm.)

I admitted something to God. I told him my prayers about my love and gratitude toward my family and friends were true, but deep inside of me I wanted to include myself. Knowing I caused my own mess and hurt others, I wasn't sure I deserved God's help, nor did I want to appear selfish. But deep down I knew God already knew this. Truthfully, after I confessed this, I felt better. He said, "It's okay. The truth will always set you free, Holly." Feeling compelled to make what I wanted clear to God, I decided to ask—knowing he is the judge, not me—and I surrendered the fear of appearing selfish. I closed my bible and blew out my candle, feeling relieved.

It takes faith and courage to let go. It can be scary, but it's not fatal. If you don't like it, you can always go back to controlling everything! I try very hard to walk on the right path, and if it is, God will let it be known. If not, God will show me something better or redirect my steps. It's up to me to keep it moving.

If you are curious about how to pray, that's awesome! Something is stirring you now. Prayer is not about taking control or trying to manipulate God to get what you want. It's about forming a relationship. While God doesn't change, he changes you.

Have a conversation with him the way you would talk to a close friend. He is the best listener, no appointment necessary, open twenty-four hours a day, and the price is free. You will know when he is in the room with you; he spends time in your heart. There might be times you don't feel as if he's in the room with you, and believe me, I know what it feels like. Sometimes I scream loudly, "Are you there? I know you are there!" He knows.

Spending time in my sanctuary is my favorite part of the day. It brings me peace, rejuvenation, endurance, and motivation. Share your time with God. I know he likes coffee! It wouldn't surprise me if he was a good dancer too.

chapter twenty-two

Inspiration and Wisdom

Since coming home, I've been struck by the number of inspirational quotes floating around—I see them on Facebook, Twitter, and LinkedIn, daily. Is it because people have it, want it, or need it? Maybe we cannot live without it. Who are these people, and why are they posting this? Do they need inspiration, are they cured, or are they trying to inspire others? In prison we had inspiration, but we did not have to post anything to social media. We used eye-to-eye contact, words, or time—time at the picnic table, time in the line, time waiting to see a nurse, lots of time.

The world will be full of inspirational quotes for as long as life is full of opposition—birth and death, young and old, love and hate, rich and poor, sunrise and sunset, believers and non-believers. The wise words stir and challenge us, and the best ones open our hearts. We sigh, we laugh, we think, and sometimes we make changes. But I cannot remember all the inspirational quotes I've read. Only a few have stuck with me.

While inspiration is great, suffering develops wisdom. What if we could find a way to hold our own joy and inspiration through our own personal stories? What about wisdom? Do people who are considered wise need inspiration? Do wise people post stuff all over social media? What is wisdom? Can anyone become wise? Are you born wise—is it genetic or something you gain? Do people regarded as wise think of themselves as wise?

Since life is full of opposition, what is the opposite of wisdom? Perhaps it is speaking or acting stupidly and then blaming others for what happens; speaking or acting in ways that cause difficulties for people or groups important to you or that lead to unnecessary loss; not learning from mistakes and making them again; being out of touch with what is happening around you; being bitter about the past or cynical about the future; being outspoken about what others are doing wrong; or acting in ways contrary to one's stated values and goals, and not knowing it.

Wise people have found a way to be happy rather than hostile, no matter how badly life has treated them. Wise people have accurate, perceptive insights into human behavior and understand how things work. They are observers of human nature, people, trees, strangers, and waterfalls. Real life experiences have been their teachers, not academic study. They don't find the need to be right or the best, and they don't mind keeping what they know to themselves but are willing to share what they know with certain individuals. They are available to give advice to open-minded learners. They have a way of asking questions that lead to new discoveries, less judgment, and more understanding. They are self-aware.

Wise people are smart about what they do and don't do. They have an inner framework of knowing without the need to examine the reasons. They "read" situations well and understand others with complete acceptance. Wise people trust and obey their intuition. Wisdom provides a radar that can sniff out hidden motives behind the actions of others. Wise people are less vulnerable to cons, threats, criticism, and manipulators. Wise people do not get worked up easily and have a way of handling pressure with humor. They remain stable in times of turmoil. They feel optimistic and self-confident even when coping with less-desirable circumstances.

Sometimes the hard times in my life have served me well, although I didn't know until I got through the hard time. Time in prison is maddening and depressing and felt unfair. But through this time, I cultivated patience. All the while something delicious, nourishing, and tasty was being prepared; however, I was not aware until afterward. Asking questions, while engaging in active listening with an open heart to understand (not debate), came easily for me while in prison. Staying objective rather than judging created an opening for me to learn. But I didn't find wisdom or manufacture it—it was given.

I thought wisdom meant having greater insight and was reserved for an exclusive group of people, people who knew how to make sound choices, academic people. Another group was the aging community. I was told I would become wiser as I aged. I don't believe this to be true anymore. I know highly intelligent people and extremely old people who would not be described as wise or insightful, but prejudiced, anxious, egotistical, and entitled.

Intellect, age, and experience shape us, but don't necessarily give wisdom. During my troubles, I leaned on the Lord and sought understanding, constantly! Never did I ask for wisdom, but it was given by the Lord.

Nothing against inspiration—I like it too!

If I had known what
I know now, I would
have been looking for
a personal revolution
instead of some silly
resolution, which I
would have forgotten
by February.

chapter twenty-three

My New Year's Revolution

I get sick and tired of hearing about New Year's resolutions—that customary list of wishes or lofty goals that are soon forgotten until the next year rolls around. Instead of losing weight or getting a promotion, new car, or bigger house, what about a life of inner character? Personally, a New Year's Resolution doesn't have to begin in January. Mine was a revolution and began on a random day after hitting rock bottom.

If I had known what I know now, I would have been looking for a personal revolution instead of some silly resolution, which I would have forgotten by February.

My dumb decisions became the icebreaker to my own inner character. Giving up the security of who I thought I was all my life pushed me into a scary place to meet myself at the core. And trust me, I did not always like who I was meeting. Blind spots will bite you hard.

The conflicts and struggles of my successful daily life were behind me. No longer was I listening to people complain and expect more of me. No longer was I trying to be super woman or witness how bitchy I can be.

In my quiet place, I was unimpressed with myself and didn't care about proving anything to the world. There was a joy in practicing humility, intentional listening, and acceptance. My personal struggle led me to the depths of my own soul.

Today, (for the most part) I am a happy soul, a silly soul. My life is not one of failure, but of an inner peace. My need to climb the ladder of success has been redirected to seek a life of balance.

My New Year's Revolution will never be forgotten.

chapter twenty-four

Intentional Listening

Have you ever felt the presence of someone really listening to you? I remember standing on the stage in the prison chapel. I wasn't sure what to talk about other than my own personal, messed-up life. Luckily, I had fond family memories.

It was early in the morning, and I stood center stage in my zookeeper uniform, the prison khakis. With many pairs of eyes staring at me, I couldn't help thinking to myself, "What the hell are you doing here?" I knew where I was but still couldn't believe I was in prison.

Every week different women would present the morning announcements, consisting of the weather, the menu, and a joke. Some were grouped together to engage audience participation in games or quizzes or expressing their favorite quotes or philosophies. On one particular day, I was assigned to share my "personal philosophy." I didn't exactly have a personal philosophy that sounded very deep, like bearing-the-soul deep. Would they laugh at me? It seemed humiliating and stupid.

Wrestling with my personal feelings and simultaneously digging for the right words to express myself, I was squeezed with anxiety, terrified to say what I really wanted to say for fear I would find myself in hot water. Could this be a setup or a test? Should I say what was expected of me or speak from my heart? And why did my heart seem so willing?

Throwing caution to the wind—or maybe it was my ego I threw to the wind—I gradually began to reveal my private thoughts, steadily one after another. The Chapel became extraordinarily silent. Were they really listening to me?

I gently began to feel a sense of calm and then of safety. I would describe it as serenity. It was as though my heart unlocked and then opened wide, while shredding parts I had held prisoner for too long. I could hear the words I spoke, not as a speaker but as a listener. It was an outpouring of my personal expression in words I was comfortable with, not perfect words but my heartfelt words. I no longer felt encumbered with anxiety but embraced my own vulnerability.

Unraveling my feelings as I cautiously exposed myself in the prison chapel that morning, I felt stirred to redirect my focus to the eyes and hearts of the other women. Some were motionless. Some nodded with understanding or agreement. Others tried to conceal their own personal exposure with sniffles, while countless others let tears fall along with mine. Part of my healing was giving up and resisting the impulse to defend. As parts of me died, finer parts came to life.

I learned by living in a prison that although we are all different and unique, we are exceedingly more alike. We had families, children young and old, husbands, relationships, friends, and lost friends. We also had unresolved struggles, horrible mistakes, shame, guilt, loneliness, and a longing to be free. We were anxious and fearful of our futures. I spoke about my passion for hope and embracing the unknown with faith and enthusiasm.

One of my favorite Mother Teresa quotes: "Spread the love of God through your life but only use words when necessary." Amen, sister!

Upon my release, I continually shared stories of my days in prison and how I was intrigued with the different lifestyles between the inside world and the outside world. Even though I was thrilled to be out of prison, I realized I had developed fond memories and didn't want to forget them. I found the outside world extremely distracting, busy, and superficial.

My boys and their girlfriends met me at a nearby restaurant shortly after I was released. After the normal chit chat and some light talk about nothing, I asked if anyone had ever thought about listening skills. Of course, they looked at me as if I were hallucinating or demented.

I explained, I had been reminiscing earlier that day about the time I revealed my heart in the prison chapel. They all looked at me and then at one another with deep concern as if I were certifiably nuts.

I felt the ladies in prison listened with greater intention than the people on the outside. It seemed people were too preoccupied, tuned out, uninterested, or ready to prove me wrong. Even those I was close to were concentrating on what they were going to say next. And how about the one who constantly interrupts because they have something far more important to say? I came to believe that "intentional listening" was becoming extinct.

People who know me well are not surprised when I pose strange questions, so I simply asked the dinner table if anyone felt there was a difference between male and female listening. Laughing out loud, the girlfriends jumped on it. They were ready to bust chops, and my sons knew it. "They fake listen!" Pretending to be stunned, I said, "Fake listen? What's that?"

About that time, the male server started chuckling as he was getting ready to take our orders. Something tells me he was listening! Most men only take note for short periods of time unless they are paying attention to sports or something they're interested in. Rocky said there are times his girlfriend is talking, and he simply responds by telling her, "I'm in my nothing box right now." That translates to, "I'm not listening to you."

My younger son's girlfriend said, "When I share a problem with Zico, I'm not asking him to solve my problem. I want him to listen and understand me. Then he starts giving advice, then we debate, or worse, it escalates into an argument. My whole need for him to listen turns into me listening to all my past mistakes."

"Why do women need to talk so much? Where's the server?"

It was a funny conversation, but the lack of awareness of the importance of truly listening was much deeper than genders. When I find myself *truly* listening, I receive insight about the person speaking as well as myself. There are times when my internal monologue can be disturbing, especially when I hear myself say, "I wish they would stop talking, so I can say something."

Skillful listening has become a practice for me. It is more than looking at someone's eyes; it is a deliberate consciousness. Active listening is not always easy, and I must remember to downshift my "to do" list and purposefully upshift my mental ones. When nothing else is in the room but me and the other person, I find I am fully present with the conversation, which seems magnified and powerful. I refuse to let those distracting feelings of rushing, interrupting, or anxiousness seep into my head. Instead, I am a participant in a compassionate exchange of humanity and dignity.

Intended listening is hard work for me and can be time-consuming (especially when I am listening to my oldest son talk—geez). It's a privilege for me to be an intentional listener. It's staying objective that I am able to let go of the need to defend or put down, no matter what I hear. I didn't say it was always easy for me to exercise restraint, especially when things become personal. Sometimes I have to bite my own fist.

When I listen with an open mind, I become a deliberate listener. This might sound silly, but I like to merge the audible sounds I hear into meaning. My heart opens with patience and something I would not have thought of myself, but I feel kind. Not only do I "ear hear" what is being said, I also hear what is not being said, which typically prompts me to give encouragement.

The old Holly was a horrible listener, too busy, frenzied, and distracted. I admit my internal monologue, my ego, was powerful and hated to lose. As a busy real estate agent and mother, my disruptions rarely stopped. Some nights I could barely sleep trying to keep up with all the conversations in my head. Now I understand why nine million people take sleep aids, although I find good wine does the same trick.

My life prior to prison got in the way of receiving what I needed to hear. My taxing schedule, a booming business, not enough time, overcrowded places, and loud conversations—all got in the way. Prison gave me space to become a captivated listener. I had plenty of time, no business, and nothing else to do. I craved conversation in long lines, waiting for a shower, or walking with another inmate. Hell, I even enjoyed talking with some of the guards.

Now I understand Proverbs 15:4 (NIV): "The soothing tongue is a tree of life." It does not say a tongue that lashes out, interrupts, accuses, and scolds is noble, nor the tongue that plays judge and director by telling people what they should or shouldn't do with their lives is soothing. I battle with my ego daily, but now I am watching for it.

I have noticed when I am in high-level listener mode, I feel more in charge of myself and experience less stress. Contentment, wholeness, and satisfaction are some benefits I have valued while actively listening, and maybe, just maybe, I have become a joy for others to be around. It's nice when people welcome me into their lives.

I know what it feels like to be heard, really heard. Intentional listeners are special people, and some remain in prison.

Staying mentally free,
while I am physically
free, is the highest
form of freedom.

chapter twenty-five

Mentally and Physically Free

Now that I am home, I am different; I think differently. I continually protect and nurture my thoughts, consciously shielding myself from the pressures of societal expectations, being right, being great, or being popular or successful. All those things can be so encompassing and restricting; they choke me. Choosing to stay alert and monitor my own thoughts is my own personal free vacation. Staying mentally free, while I am physically free, is the highest form of freedom. You can be mentally confined while lying on the beach or mentally free while cleaning toilets.

Are you easily agitated or frequently stressed out? The longer I am out of prison, the more I am aware of these feelings. Being free means I have the freedom to choose. "Choose" is the operative word. Choose everything—what I do, how I act, how I react, how I think, how I process my thoughts. I have freedom to choose happiness as well as freedom to act like a jerk.

A person who is locked up has very little freedom and over time will adjust to managing the little freedoms they are given.

For example, we were free to choose what books we wanted to read in the outdated library. I could stand in front of the romance section and scan all twenty-three used books. You might think "only twenty-three." Well, there were some advantages to that—it was easy to make a choice. Rarely did I get overwhelmed with the selection. It wasn't like selecting crackers from the grocery store—OMG, sea salt, rosemary and olive oil, cracked black pepper, reduced fat, original, brown rice, roasted garlic, sweet onion, sweet potato, red bean—enough already!

After I read a book, I would return the "more used book" and then check out another one. It was easy to keep track of what I had read and what awaited me, unlike Netflix. My list, continue watching, new releases, or trending now—we have so many options, I find myself uncertain about whether I've seen a movie or not. With an abundance of options comes confusion. I didn't have chaos like that in prison. I knew exactly what I had read.

I turned a movie on one night, and it looked familiar, but I wasn't sure. I felt as if I had seen parts of the movie, but did I ever finish it? If I did, was it good? If it was good, why can't I remember? Do I invest my time and watch it again? Jeez, what to do, what to do? Would it be a waste of my time to watch it again, or does this mean I ought to try it again and maybe I will remember it this time? These feelings were not comforting.

Having a variety of choices is appealing, but it can also be overwhelming. I found it easier to make decisions in the prison commissary than at the grocery store today. I didn't always like the assortment, but I learned to be grateful for what was there. Colgate or Crest—pick one or pick both if you can't decide, but then you might not have enough money for Cheetos. I preferred Crest, and sometimes the prison had Crest 3D for whitening, although it was more expensive than the others, but if my teeth were white I felt better. (Weirdo me.)

The simplification of alternatives made our choices easy, simple, and straightforward. Life, as you and I know today, is full of diverse tastes, colors, gadgets, passwords, organizations, meetup groups, shoe stores, calorie counters—sometimes it's just too much. I've found myself in situations where it's easier to walk away and have a glass of wine instead.

In prison, I didn't have the freedom to choose my job, clothing, or meals, and the rules were not created by popular vote. We were told where to go, where to report, when to return, and when escape charges were issued. I knew what the expectations were and didn't try to revise the orders. I adapted. Didn't mean I liked it!

Listening to people complain, worry, and fret over advantageous decisions—where to make dinner reservations, whether to order the chef's special or the filet, whether to visit the cabin for the weekend or an entire week, whether to drive the family car or the toy car—it never ends.

We ate what was served without stress, even though it was at best revolting. Deciding on what car to drive is never an issue for the incarcerated. Nor are car maintenance, traffic jams, gas pumps, or car washes. My feet were my wheels. The idea of having two feet took on a whole new meaning, especially the importance of taking care of them. Keeping my ten toes pleasantly cushioned with appropriate socks similar to the treads on your tires, daily cleaning and drying like the car wash, and free from gravel or foreign objects. Occasionally little pebbles would work their way into my shoes, especially my first pair, which were used by another inmate, holes and all.

My take-it-for-granted attitude before prison changed to gratitude for life, nature's fragrances in the dewy morning air, the distinguishable chirps of the little birds waking up, watching the dark become daybreak, and passing other ladies and joyfully saying, "Good morning." I felt pleased and richly rewarded to experience my five senses. I could see, hear, smell, taste, and touch. It was all so magnified while in prison. I didn't want to lose it or forget it.

My desire was to do something greater with my uneventful hours. Even though I couldn't see time, hear it, smell it, taste it, or touch it, I knew it was there. Time had a purpose. I had a purpose.

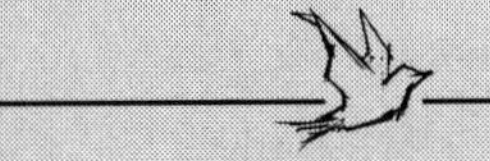

The ego and the Holy
Spirit will argue,
and ego doesn't like
to lose—this is the
human experience.

chapter twenty-six

God's Homing Device

I remember my first adult beverage. I sat in the back seat of a yellow Chevy Nova with a black interior. I wasn't concerned with our destination but felt slightly conflicted, sensing I was about to experience something for the first time. The sensation of excitement mixed with fear created a symphony of mixed signals in my brain.

A part of me wanted to be home eating popcorn in my pajamas. Sometimes my mom would buy soda, and I could float ice cream in it. Cream soda was my favorite. The vision of being with my family gave me comfort and security, reminded me of the *Little House on the Prairie*. I was not feeling comfortable and secure in the back seat of the yellow Nova.

Certainly, I could act like I didn't notice, but that wouldn't be very convincing since there were two other people sitting next to me and three others in the front seat. I could try pulling the sick card, but they would probably think I was a baby or immature. It was supposed to be fun and was appropriate for my age group. One cold beer later, I thought, "This must be what it feels like to be drunk. I'm all grown up, but this is wrong." After the second beer, I got scared and told my friends to take me home. The first beer was my own temptation; the second beer was God's grace.

I became very intrigued and intoxicated with the Holy Spirit while I was under lock and key. I wanted to understand how I ended up in prison—what did I miss? Where was my discernment? Clearly, my antenna was broken. Have you ever had a bad feeling about a situation? What did you do when you got that feeling? Did you proceed? Did you convince yourself everything was okay? Please be honest with yourself.

Friends would ask, "Holly, didn't you know? Didn't you have a feeling?" For years I kept saying, no, I don't think so. Then while I was lying in Cube 44, I realized I clearly had a sense something was wrong; I remember telling him I would lose my license if I paid him a referral fee. So, yes, I did hear, but I did not obey. Instead, I neglected to make the right decision and justified my ego. When I look back (hindsight is 20/20), I can see now.

The ego and the Holy Spirit will argue, and ego doesn't like to lose—this is the human experience. Through a critical thinking error, I created my own slippery slope. I had an overpowering self.

I like to look at it like this: between God and the human experience is an infinite gap, the Holy Spirit. God's plan was to plant a little bit of himself inside of us. This is our homing device, radar, navigation system, third eye, intuition—whatever you want to call it, we all have it. Romans 5:5 (NIV) says, "The love of God has been poured into our hearts by the Holy Spirit, which has been given to us."

This is fantastic news for today and every day. It's not something you read and then go back to your cranky, prideful self. (Do you get what I'm saying?) Practice this, read it, and reread it. If we don't put the Word into us mentally, we will never be able to practice it physically. The love of God is in us, and we give it back to God by loving our neighbors and enemies alike.

Check your attitudes and actions to know whether you're being led by the Spirit. Galatians 5:22–23 (ESV) says, "The fruit of the Spirit is love, joy, peace, patience, kindness, goodness, faithfulness, gentleness, and self-control." Are these things evident in your life? If you want an honest answer, ask someone who doesn't fear speaking the truth, at all costs. This is only a hint, but if you are being led by the Spirit, people will notice and some will tell you. That is your testimony!

Even though I spend a lot of time alone, rarely do I feel lonely. My very best friend lives inside me, and we go everywhere together. We talk to each other often, and surprisingly, at times we agree. The voice that lives inside of me has a great sense of humor. I put new meaning in the phrase "LOL" because I really do laugh out loud!

Sometimes I wake up in the middle of the night recognizing my own voice. Generally, it's my mind reminding me of things I need to do the next day. However, my friend has a way of rolling me over and calming my mind down. I begin to breathe deeper while thanking God for gazing upon me. When I wake up in the morning, I recall the event, stretching my arms out wide and thanking God for the gift of sleep.

When I decide to listen to the inner voice that is not my own, things turn out better.

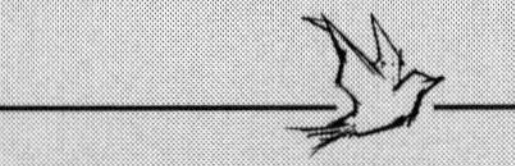

I've had to accept my losses, and now I'm classified as a felon. My new classification certainly does not define who I am—don't let titles fool you.

chapter twenty-seven

My Final Lesson

When the red phone rang, the range would get alarmingly quiet. Sometimes it meant there was a visitor or a guard or counselor looking for you, or maybe the chaplain, which could be good or bad news. The absolute best times were when someone was getting released. I knew it was a big mistake for me to be in prison and knew the red phone would ring at any minute for my automatic release. Early on, every time I heard the phone ring, I would stop dead in my tracks, my eyes locked on the red phone. Over time, the red phone continued ringing, and I found myself not paying any attention any more. My automatic release wasn't coming after all.

I fell into a routine of getting up every morning fifteen minutes before the guards did their rounds to put hot water in my mug for my instant coffee. Propping myself against the cinderblock wall with my bible, journal, pen, and highlighter one morning, I recalled when my pastor compared me to a burned house. "Yes, Holly, you have burned down, but you still have your foundation." That morning in Cube 44 I decided to exchange my cube for a classroom. I begged God not to let me be released and returned home until I understood why, why I had said yes.

There was a problem: Albert Einstein and I are close friends. I am sure if he were here today, we would be official Facebook friends. I heard Albert say to me, "We cannot solve our problems with the same thinking we used when we created them." I knew I was going to need help.

The fight to avoid prison was over for me. Even though I had physically surrendered, I hadn't mentally. I used to pretend I was filming a documentary as my way of escaping. The more I continued to film my documentary without judgment, the more peaceful I became. I liked stepping away from myself while my thoughts were only observational. I had no attachment to the outcome of the things I observed. Developing a practice of objectivity gave me an awareness of contentment. Soon it became apparent to me that I was mentally surrendering and viewing the world through a different colored lens, and I liked it.

Let me give you an example. Two inmates are sitting at a picnic table. They're whispering, talking, and even laughing. It's a sunny day, and I walk over to join them. As soon as I am in front of them, they stop talking and laughing. They seem different.

If this scenario had happened before prison, I might've wondered why they stopped talking. What is it they don't want me to know? Were they talking about me? But prison taught me to remain neutral. All I really know is two people were talking and stopped when I walked up.

Living in a controlled environment helped me to locate something nobody could control: my thoughts. Controlling my personal feelings and thinking was an introduction to my best buddy. Friends take care of one another, so I had to take care of my new views. I hated my circumstances but found peace despite being in a prison. Contentment is never based on circumstances; it's from the inside, and I liked living a new way of appreciating.

I thought back on how I ended up in prison. Someone I knew asked me to pay him a referral fee after he brought a buyer to one of my listings, and I paid it. That doesn't sound like a terrible thing, except for the fact he wasn't a licensed real estate agent. In the world of real estate, you're only permitted to pay a referral fee to another licensed agent. I was surprised when he asked me to do it. I asked him if he was licensed. When he said no, I distinctly remember telling him I could lose my license if I paid the fee. Then he went on to explain that it wasn't technically a referral fee, but a consulting fee. He wasn't referring his clients to me personally, but he was investing time consulting them on whether the purchase would be a good investment for them. It seemed to make sense. He then suggested he would bill my company a consulting fee. I wasn't thrilled with the idea of paying him a fee, but I did. It was a critical-thinking error.

I felt some of his behaviors were odd, but I didn't stop to examine my suspicion. I looked up to him because he had come from another country and was successful (or so I thought). I thought he must be smarter than me because I was only a real estate agent. Sometimes we do not see people as *they* are; we see things as *we* are. During my professional career, I was considered extremely motivated, enthusiastic, passionate, disciplined, organized, and consistent. And I was a people pleaser. I didn't want to disappoint him.

My critical-thinking errors didn't just happen. It wasn't like *bam*, and I was caught. These thinking errors probably started in high school. I was the captain of the cheerleading squad, voted most athletic, served on the student council, and was homecoming princess. I knew right from wrong but measured my self-worth based on how others perceived me. When we do this, we risk compromise. My decision was a critical-thinking error, not realizing he was orchestrating a large mortgage-fraud ring. But ignorance is not a defense.

I had heard the word codependent, but didn't like the sound of it, especially since I prided myself on being independent. What I learned, however, was that I put myself in harm's way at the risk of helping someone else. I helped him to further his fraud. I now call it stupid.

Let's pretend your boss calls you up while you're at the office, and he is enjoying his day on the golf course at his country club. Your boss is successful, well respected, and admired by many. He asks you to sign a legal document because he overlooked a place where his signature was required. You are not sure what to do. He says, "Thanks for being a team player," and hangs up the phone.

Now what? Maybe you're thinking, "Well, he asked me to do this, so it's probably OK. I don't want to mess up the sale. I want to be a team player. He's a successful man—knows what needs to be done." So what do you do? You sign it! Did you risk compromise? Did you fear disappointing him? Did you commit forgery? Is that fraud? Can you go to prison for that?

One day, this person (who I thought was a friend and trustworthy professional) handed me a commission check, and I asked, "Why are you giving that to me?" It made no sense until I rationalized it. He said it was his way of thanking me for all the hours showing him property. He said everybody had agreed, and it was OK. He was right—I had spent a lot of time with him. I began feeling a sense of entitlement—another critical thinking error. My ego voice said I deserved that check.

I had heard other agents received commission checks when they had not been part of the real estate transaction and thought it was my lucky day. I blamed others. I accepted the check because others had. Besides, he said he was only trying to be nice. He said he knew many agents, but out of all the agents, he thought I worked the hardest and knew I was the single mother. He made me feel as if he cared about me. What's wrong with being nice? He played to the sentimental part of my decision-making, my heart.

Have you ever felt like you deserved something or perhaps were entitled to something? Let's try this. You come back from the grocery store. As you're going through your wallet, you notice you received too much change back from the cashier. You begin to hear voices: "Oh, man, they gave me too much money back. I don't feel like getting in the car and driving through the traffic and the heat. They probably won't even know the money is missing. I spend massive amounts of money in that store, maybe this is just my lucky day. They've probably overcharged me before, and I probably never noticed. We'll just call it even." Does this sound familiar? What do you do?

No one wants to go to prison, but does anybody ever think about the possibility? I never did, but I do now, all the time!

My father is a West Point graduate and often shares stories with me about his days as a young cadet. Not long ago, I sat on his back deck listening to his endless stories. My father is not much of a praying man, but he told me they had what is known as the cadet prayer. Part of that prayer says, "Make us to choose the harder right rather than the easier wrong." I suppose if it were so easy to do, it would not be part of a prayer. I believe I chose the easier wrong.

Another subject I became captivated with while in prison was intuition, something we all have in common. My friends would ask me if I had any idea my friend was committing fraud. "Holly, did you have any signs, any feelings, anything?" For a long time, I said no, nothing. But when I took the time to really think about it, I did think he was strange, I did get a feeling, but I didn't take caution to it. Intuition functions so quickly and so well that sometimes we don't notice it.

Had I taken the time to listen to what I was hearing, at least enough time to process and discern what was going on, it may have saved me from telling this story. Perhaps I just wanted to believe what I wanted to believe?

Filing taxes are painful. Most of us do not enjoy paying the government, and sometimes we use our fuzzy calculators. How many lunches were truly company related? What voices did you hear when you claimed those deductions? Did you hear the saint or the sinner? I know we don't think of ourselves as saints or sinners, but we do hear conflicting voices. Did you listen to your protector, your guide, your navigator, your helper, your free defense attorney? Or did you listen to your pride, your greed, your jealousy, your ego? It's human nature.

When you're not sure what voice to follow, sometimes it's

best to listen to the voice that's not your own. Be careful—the ego voice hates to lose. Before I was aware of anything, I had a wonderful life. As a matter of fact, I wanted to sleep quickly because I was eager to open my eyes again each morning. I earned a substantial income. I lived in million-dollar homes, dined in upscale restaurants, drove luxury cars, and sipped only the finest wines.

Today, I have a life—a good life. I sleep well, and I'm grateful. I live in a very tiny townhouse, I rarely dine out, I do not drive a luxury car, but I have acquired a taste for wine under $10 a bottle. I stand before you as a reminder that the downside risk caused by my bad decision was far greater than the upside benefits accrued from all my good ones.

The day I was released, I felt like a new listing! I've had to accept my losses, and now I'm classified as a felon. My new designation certainly does not define who I am—don't let titles fool you. For all the times I wanted to die or felt like I died, never were they fatal. My sentence was a path to my own personal freedom, and I'm grateful for the trip.

After my release, one of my girlfriends gave me a very special gift, a teacup. She had hunted for a long time to find the perfect present. While she was admiring the teacup, the salesperson quickly disclosed a flaw—a chip on the rim. It's still very beautiful and purposeful.

The teacup today sits on a stack of well-read books admirably displayed in my living room. The chip on the rim is my thorn, my prison. It's so miniscule compared to the rest of the intricate details of the little teacup. Learning to love myself, flaws and all, has helped me to love others' imperfections as well. It was hardly a joy ride, but it helped me to find the peacefulness and joy in my own life.

Not all prisons are so literal. In fact, I'd bet you dinner for two there are more people living in mental prisons than actual prisons. The pain, suffering, or blame and the yearning to hold on to the chip can keep one locked up. Yes, the consequence of our choices can be brutal, alarming, and downright dumb, but hopefully not terminal. Freedom is creating a mindfulness that we can select what we think. Nobody can take that away. Understanding the voices ping ponging in our head can give us direction, but we must be alert to critical thinking and quieting that damn ego.

About the Author

Holly Pasut was a nationally recognized real estate agent in the booming southeast market. Personality and relationship building led her to be among the top agents in the country. Then she was sentenced to federal prison for twenty-one months for involvement in a mortgage fraud case that was one of the largest investigations in the United States. She was released after serving only thirteen months.

She shares the story of her path from an iconic agent to a federal prison cell with white-collar professionals and university students around the country. Her audiences are awakened to the risks professionals take often without even knowing it. Topics include big lessons from federal prison, critical thinking errors, recognizing your inner voice, and changing your mindset.

A life group leader, certified life coach, and certified volunteer for several ministries and second chance organizations, Holly encourages socially stigmatized groups to live beyond their stigma. She is a loving mother to three adult children who inspire her on a daily basis. Quiet early morning meditations are part of her spiritual regime, along with regular work outs and long walks, and she is easily distracted by music.

Connect with Holly

FreedomSpeaker.com
holly@freedomspeaker.com
FreedomSpeakerHolly
pasutholly

Invite Holly Pasut, the Freedom Speaker, to keynote your upcoming event.

Our culture respects higher education and strong work ethics, and we often admire those at the top, especially when the competition is fierce. What happens when an educated, successful professional makes a bad decision? Learn how the downside risks caused by bad decisions are far greater than the upside benefits accrued by all the good ones!

Visit FreedomSpeaker.com for more information.

Made in the USA
Columbia, SC
16 September 2019